Advance Praise for DEFEATING SIN: Overcoming our Passions and Changing Forever:

"Fr. Joseph Huneycutt's book, *DEFEATING SIN: Overcoming our Passions and Changing Forever*, provides a deep exploration of the Passions and the Virtues. It is also serves as a wonderful spiritual tool for making a good Confession. Fr. Joseph's work was implemented at Camp St. Thekla, where we used the concept in our Christian Education program. The campers and staff were blessed to be able to come to a deeper understanding of the Passions and Virtues and learn how to make a more meaningful and full Confession. Even the youngest of campers enjoyed this program, and especially found the Meditations in the book inspiring. I highly recommend Fr. Joseph's book to anyone looking for a spiritual aid to help them on the constant journey to Repentance."

-- Ashley Kevorkian, Camp St Thekla Christian Education Director, 2005

"Father Joseph has the unusual ability to take timeless truth, Biblical knowledge, and theology, and communicate them in a practical and readily understandable form that has the wonderful potential of helping us to be transformed through the renewing of our minds."

-- Ron Ephrem Moore, International Singer/Songwriter/Speaker

"Passions and Virtues – words not generally used in everyday vocabulary in the 21st century. Yet, who of us has not seen lives ruined or exalted as a direct result of one or the other of these words and their implications. This book provides meaningful and practical insight into the significant "opposites" that affect our lives both here and hereafter. Fr. Joseph takes us to that fateful garden where the first Adam, the first Eve and the first tree set a course for death and destruction. But he also takes us to a hill where the second Adam, the second Eve and a very different tree changes that course for eternity. Read this, go to Confession, and then read it again."

-- *John Maddex, General Manager, Ancient Faith Radio*

"This book is like a treasure chest filled with gems of wisdom from the Fathers and Theologians of the Church. Each of these jewels help give insight to the common reader on the Fall of man, the Passions, the Virtues, Spiritual Warfare and the way toward Repentance. Fr. Joseph, in his warm personal style, not only attempts to give us a theological understanding of the themes but provides practical helps in the form of definitions, prayers, and inspirational Meditations. These tools are great assets to have for those who are seeking to apply the material in order to struggle against the Passions, aspire to the Virtues, and properly prepare for the sacrament of Repentance. A great resource for self examination!"

-- *Constantine Shepherd, Youth Director, Annunciation Greek Orthodox Church, Winston-Salem, North Carolina*

"This attractive exposition of current, yet timeless, anthropological issues is distinguished by its clarity of vision and originality of expression. As the book unfolds, it becomes increasingly evident that the unbroken Tradition of the Church is the sole key to understanding God's revelation to man. Because the author has so firmly placed his trust in the holiness of this Tradition, his thinking, both creative and inspired, elucidates the charismatic character of the way of salvation which leads to the renewal of life. His doctrine is sound, and it will surely prove to be of great value in informing and convincing the heart of modern man about God's truth."

-- *Archimandrite Zacharias (Zacharou), Patriarchal Stavropegic Monastery of St John the Baptist, Essex, England*

"*Defeating Sin*, like its author Fr. Joseph Huneycutt, is a fantastic combination of Holy Orthodoxy and wit in 21st century clothing. I recommend it highly for those who seek a primer on how to deepen their own Repentance."

-- *Archpriest Josiah Trenham, Ph.D., St. Andrew Antiochian Orthodox Church, Riverside, California*

"The new book *Defeating Sin*, by Fr Joseph Huneycutt is an ambitious project which tackles a difficult and complex topic with seeming ease. The topic of the Passions occupies many pages of writings by a multitude of Church Fathers and is one of the more difficult to grasp completely. Fr Joseph has done a masterful job of collecting some of these writings and by weaving together excerpts from Fathers both ancient and modern with commentary of his own, he presents a tapestry that is clear, concise and within the grasp of most readers. He has indeed taken a complex topic and made it very understandable. His presentation is also more than simply an academic treatise on the Passions for he weaves in throughout a pastoral understanding of how to use this knowledge in the process of spiritual growth. In reading this book I was inspired by the clear and yet deep picture of the Passions, how they affect our lives and how we can conquer them in our own lives.

I would recommend this book as an important part of the library of any Orthodox Christian, and particularly as a resource for pastors as they strive to shepherd their flock into the safe fold of the Kingdom of God."

-- Archpriest David Moser, St Seraphim of Sarov Russian Orthodox Church, Boise, Idaho

"This book has evolved over several decades of reflection that is both personal and part of our Orthodox family inheritance. This is a read that will bring many back through its pages just as memories of powerful retreats and epiphanies return to us and become once again moments of grace in an hour of need. *DEFEATING SIN: Overcoming our Passions and Changing Forever* is a book that will be marked up and well-worn by those who own it and no doubt shared with other Christians who long for a well of renewal and a blessed retreat."

-- The Very Rev. Dr. Chad Hatfield, Chancellor, St. Vladimir's Orthodox Seminary

DEFEATING SIN
Overcoming our Passions and Changing Forever

By
Fr. Joseph David Huneycutt

Preface
By
Bishop BASIL

Regina Orthodox Press
Salisbury, Massachusetts

Nativity '07

Deacon David —

May God bless you & your ministry — family with good health & many years.

IC XC

Joseph +

DEFEATING SIN:
Overcoming our Passions and Changing Forever
ISBN 978-1-928653-31-8

© 2007 Joseph David Huneycutt

Regina Orthodox Press
PO BOX 5288
Salisbury MA 01952

reginaorthodoxpress.com

For Charles

This book is dedicated to the man who first introduced me to the acronym PALE GAS and the image of the TWO TREES, the Rev'd Dr Charles Caldwell. Fr Caldwell taught at Nashotah House Episcopal Seminary where he was both revered and reviled. As it turned out, his circular reasoning and seemingly wild anecdotes ended up making perfect sense to most of us only *after* ordination and parish service.

May God save him and make more like him!

TABLE OF CONTENTS

Acknowledgements

This work began as a Lenten Retreat for Orthodox Christians in fulfillment of the requirements for a doctoral degree in the Eastern Christian Context from Pittsburgh Theological Seminary, in conjunction with the Antiochian House of Studies (1999).

I am indebted to my instructors and classmates for their love, criticism, forbearance, and fraternity; humble thanks, as well, go to the patient readers and editors of that project.

Many communities, Orthodox and other, have helped to shape this work through its various phases:

Lake Junaluska Methodist Retreat Center – Lake Junaluska, North Carolina

The Monastery of the Glorious Ascension – Resaca, Georgia

St Nicholas Orthodox Mission – Fletcher, North Carolina

Russian Orthodox Cathedral of St John the Baptist – Washington, DC

St Herman Russian Orthodox Youth Conference (1999) – Nyack, New York

St Elizabeth the New Martyr Mission – Columbia, South Carolina

St Thekla Orthodox Youth Camp (2005) – Nashville, Tennessee

St Jonah of Manchuria Russian Orthodox Mission – Spring, Texas

St Herman Seminary – Kodiak, Alaska

St Innocent Academy – Kodiak, Alaska

St George Orthodox Christian Church – Houston, Texas

St Michael Orthodox Church – Beaumont, Texas

Annunciation Greek Orthodox Church – Winston-Salem, North Carolina

Humble thanks to the following people for their help with this project in its various forms: Metropolitan Hierotheos (Vlachos), Archimandrite Daniel Griffith, Archpriest Michael Dahulich, Dr Anthony Gythiel, Priest John Salem, Susan Engelhardt, and my wife, Amy Elizabeth.

PREFACE

We confess, then, that He assumed all the natural and innocent passions of man. For He assumed the whole man and all man's attributes save sin. For that is not natural, nor is it implanted in us by the Creator, but arises voluntarily in our mode of life as the result of a further implantation by the devil, though it cannot prevail over us by force. For the natural and innocent passions are those which are not in our power, but which have entered into the life of man owing to the condemnation by reason of the transgression; such as hunger, thirst, weariness, labour, the tears, the corruption, the shrinking from death, the fear, the agony with the bloody sweat, the succour at the hands of angels because of the weakness of the nature, and other such like passions which belong by nature to every man. All, then, He assumed that He might sanctify all. — Of a truth our natural passions were in harmony with nature and above nature in Christ. For they were stirred in Him after a natural manner when He permitted the flesh to suffer what was proper to it: but they were above nature because that which was natural did not in the Lord assume command over the will. For no compulsion is contemplated in Him but all is voluntary. For it was with His will that He hungered and thirsted and feared and died.

St John of Damascus, Chapter XX of An Exact Exposition of the Orthodox Faith

Echoing the above salvific doctrine explicated for us by our Venerable and God-bearing Father John of Damascus (676-749), a bishop-elect in his First Profession of Faith publicly proclaims, "I confess that He took upon Himself all our weaknesses which accompany our nature – except sin: such as hunger, thirst, fatigue, tears and the like. Those were active in Him, though not by compulsion as in us, but through the obedience of His human will to His divine will. For He willed, and He hungered. He willed, and

vii

He thirsted. He willed, and He was fatigued. He willed, and He died." These passions called by the Damascene "natural and innocent" (or, more accurately, *unblameworthy*) are those termed by St Maximos the Confessor (580-662) the *bodily* passions – the passions which, in accordance with our prelapsarian nature, are appropriate, even blessed, when they are directed toward God.

But like Evagrius Ponticus (345-399) and St John Cassian (360-433) before him, the Confessor distinguishes between these *bodily* or natural passions and the post-lapsarian passions of the *soul*, which he refers to as the "gentiles of the soul." These passions indeed are "contrary to nature" (Centuries on Love, II, 16). What are these "gentiles of the soul?" The principal unnatural passions are gluttony, fornication, avarice, grief, anger, accidie (i.e., listlessness or sloth), vainglory, and pride.

It is with these "gentiles of the soul" – conflated sometime between AD 900 and 1000 from the eight classic patristic *Passions of the Soul* to the contemporary *Seven Vices* (Pride, Anger, Lust, Envy, Gluttony, Avarice, and Sloth - the mnemonic being "Pale Gas" which is the theological student's equivalent of the musician's "Every Good Boy Does Fine")[1] – and their opposites known collectively as the *Seven Virtues* (Humility, Patience, Chastity, Contentedness, Temperance, Liberality, and Diligence) that the present book by my spiritual son, Father Joseph Huneycutt, is concerned. And it is proper that all fourteen of these *V's* be considered together for, as the late Ivan M. Kontzevitch wrote in Chapter 2 of his classic work, *The Acquisition of the Holy Spirit in Ancient Russia*,[2] "Passions, like Virtues, are interconnected, just as 'links of a single chain' (St Isaac of Nitria), one being an offshoot

---

1 In earlier centuries the mnemonic was *Saligia* (*Superbia*-pride, *Accidia*-sloth, *Luxuria*-lust, *Invidia*-envy, *Gula*-gluttony, *Ira*-anger, and *Avaritia*-avarice), from whence the Latin verb *saligiare* (to commit a deadly sin) is taken.
2 Platina, CA: St Herman's Press, 1989.

viii

of another." As one struggles against a passion, one cannot help but simultaneously struggle to acquire a virtue.

May you, Reader, be blessed and enlightened and encouraged in your struggle by the wisdom contained in this book, to the glory of the All-holy Trinity and the salvation of your soul.

+ B A S I L
Bishop of Wichita and the Diocese of Mid-America
Antiochian Orthodox Christian Archdiocese of North America

July 5, 2007 The Commemoration of the New Martyr and Grand Duchess Elizabeth

INTRODUCTION

Opposite Day in Paradise and Beyond

There's a game that children sometimes play where the rules are reversed; it's called Opposite Day. That is, participants turn everything around and do the opposite of what is requested or expected. When it comes to the story of our Fall and Redemption, there's more to Opposite Day than first meets the eye. For, as St Paul writes: "I do not understand my own actions. For I do not do what I want, but I do the very thing I hate" (Rom. 7:15).[1]

The purpose of this book is to educate and encourage Christians in the struggles of spiritual warfare according to the teachings of the Church Fathers and contemporary theologians within a creative format. A great line from one of my favorite movies, **Amadeus**, is: "Too many notes!" Though the same might be said of the work at hand – there are a lot of notes and quotes from Saints, respected theologians, and contemporary teachers – the book is written for the common reader desiring a better understanding of repentance. As a teaching tool for public use, or for personal preparation alone, the quotes serve to show that this struggle against Passion toward Virtue is as old as the Church (at least!). In such a battle, we should not rely on our own reasoning but on those God-pleasing examples, the Saints and Fathers, who have gone before.

---

[1] Unless otherwise noted, all Scripture quotations are from *The New Oxford Annotated Bible, Revised Standard Version* (New York: Oxford University Press, 1977).

The book is not intended to be an exhaustive treatise on the subject of the Garden of Eden, the Two Trees, or the Fall of Man. Rather, readers will learn about the Passions and the corresponding Virtues using a visual metaphor of the Two Trees – the Tree of the Knowledge of Good and Evil, and the Tree of Life – found in the Book of Genesis.[2] Ultimately, this should help towards understanding repentance and in making a good confession. Fundamentally, a good confession is one in which the penitent has acquired insight into his or her shortcomings and not only confesses with contrite heart, but earnestly desires divine intervention, vowing to reverse his or her course of behavior. This is, obviously, in stark contrast to the perfunctory confession which may or may not lead to a change in one's life in Christ.

Many people do not know how to make a good confession. Also, over the past couple of decades, the Orthodox Church has received many new converts from various Christian backgrounds who have never experienced Confession (at least as we know it in the Church). While those who have been reared in the Faith may be more comfortable with the idea of confessing sins in the presence of a priest, all penitents struggle in their preparation for sacramental confession and are often unaware of the nature of their sins. There are even people, pious in every other way, who have never gone to Confession. It is my hope that this book will aid *all* in this

---

[2] There is nothing *evil* about the Tree of the Knowledge of Good and Evil. God is not the author of evil, and pronounces His creation: "Good." Yet since the transgression of our first parents involved this tree, for sake of example the image of the Tree of Knowledge of Good and Evil will be used, metaphorically, as an image of that transgression.

struggle we call Spiritual Warfare and the reconciling sacrament of Confession.

This book originally took the form of a Lenten Retreat for Orthodox Christians. While Retreats are common within Roman Catholic and Protestant gatherings, it is a medium seldom utilized within an Orthodox Christian context. It may be that the practice of guided retreats developed after the Great Schism of 1054 in the West and never caught on in the East. Or, it may be due to the small number of monastic communities in this country. There are few Orthodox monasteries in the United States; fewer still which conduct services in English. Though this number is changing, it is nevertheless a factor. While most Christians might attend a Retreat in a "Retreat Center" or a similar facility, the monastery would, traditionally, serve the same purpose for Orthodox Christians. Whatever the reason for its absence in Orthodox communities, it is my belief that a Retreat can be a worthy and beneficial exercise that bears God-pleasing fruit.

Back in seminary, I bought a book, **Hymns on Paradise**, by St Ephraim the Syrian.[3] Only three days elapsed between the purchasing and the consumption of this book; immediately following which, I burst into my Pastoral Theology Professor's office and, with great excitement, began relating to him my discovery of this gem and the metaphor of the Two Trees and our salvation. "Do you know what St Ephraim the Syrian says happened to the Tree of Life after the transgression of Adam and Eve?" I asked with exuberance. Somewhere amid my euphoria I heard him answer, "It was subsumed into the

---

[3] Ephraim, Saint, *Hymns on Paradise*, trans. Sebastian Brock (New York: St Vladimir's Seminary Press, 1990).

earth only to sprout again on Calvary?" "Yes!" I was surprised – this image being new to me, I expected it to be new to everyone!

> God had created the Tree of Life and hidden it from Adam and Eve, first, so that it should not, with its beauty, stir up conflict with them and so double their struggle, and also because it was inappropriate that they should be observant of the commandment of Him who cannot be seen for the sake of a reward that was there before their eyes.

> Under the Old Covenant the Tree of Life continued to remain hidden from humanity, and it was only with the Crucifixion that it was finally made manifest.

> Greatly saddened was the Tree of Life
> when it beheld Adam stolen away from it;
> it sank down into the virgin ground and was hidden
>   -- to burst forth and reappear on Golgotha;
> humanity, like birds that are chased,
> took refuge in it
> so that it might return them to their proper home.
> The chaser was chased away, while the doves
> That had been chased
> now hop with joy in Paradise.[4]

---

[4] HOP (Hymn on Virginity XVI.10), p. 60.

Much of this book is based on the visual paradigm of the Two Trees, one for the Passions, and the other for the Virtues. One should be led *from* the Passions[5] *to* the Virtues.[6]

---

[5] **PASSION:** In Greek, the word signifies literally that which happens to a person or thing, an experience undergone passively; hence an appetite or attribute such as anger, desire, or jealousy that violently dominates the soul. Many Greek Fathers regard the passions as something intrinsically evil, a "disease" of the soul: thus St John Climacus affirms that God is not the creator of the passions and that they are "unnatural," alien to man's true self [cf. Saint John Climacus, *The Ladder of Divine Ascent*, trans. Lazarus Moore (Boston: Holy Transfiguration Monastery, 1979), Step 26]. Other Greek Fathers, however, look on the passions as impulses originally placed in man by God, and so fundamentally good, although at present distorted by sin (cf. St Isaiah the Solitary - vol.1, p. 22). On this second view, then, the passions are to be educated, not eradicated; to be transfigured, not suppressed; to be used positively, not negatively (Sts. Nikodimos and Makarios, *The Philokalia*, trans. and ed. G.E.H. Palmer, Phillip Sherrard, Kallistos Ware (London: Faber & Faber, 1984), vol. 3, pp. 361-362).

[6] **VIRTUE:** The wisdom of the psalmist describes the virtuous man by saying that his heart is full of the law of God and takes pleasure in it (Ps.1:2; 37: 31), while the evil man has a heart that is empty of God and considers Him as nonexistent (Ps.14:1) [Xavier Leon-Dufour, *Dictionary of Biblical Theology* (New York: Seabury, 1973), p. 636].

NOTE: The Seven Capital Virtues are the opposite of the seven grievous sins: Humility, Liberality, Chastity, Mildness, Temperance, Happiness, and Diligence [Stephen Upson, *A Pocket Prayer Book for Orthodox Christians* (Englewood, New Jersey: The Antiochian Orthodox Christian Archdiocese, 1956), p. 29].

A passion is a spiritual disease that dominates the soul. When one repeatedly falls into a certain sin, it becomes second nature – a passion – for him to keep falling into that sin. Thus, one who misuses the God-given powers of the soul of desire and anger, or one who continually succumbs to temptations of lust, hate, malice, or jealousy, or one who subscribes to vainglory, acquires those passions.[7]

Then there's the problem that I encountered in the beginning stages of this project in 1997. I attended a presentation by Metropolitan Hierotheos (Vlachos), who refers to the Two Trees frequently in his writings. As I listened to his presentation, I was struck by his stating that Man was created *with* the Passions! "No, no, no!" I thought; not that I distrusted His Eminence's exposition of Patristic Theology, quite the contrary! It's just that my doctoral project was centered on metanoia[8] – making a u-turn – from the Passions to the Virtues. Part of the premise from which I had been working insisted that Man was created *without* the Passions; thus, the Passions were a result of the Fall.

I should elaborate that, in the scheme of the Retreat, the Two Trees serve as opposites. In other words, upon the Forbidden Tree hangs a Serpent (incarnate evil) and the fruits of the Passions; upon the Tree of Life hangs the body of the crucified Incarnate God and the Virtues.

---

[7] Elder Joseph the Hesychast, *Monastic Wisdom* (Florence, Arizona: St Anthony's Greek Orthodox Monastery, 1998), p. 403.

[8] A change of mind; a turn-around; repentance.

The project describes the "process" of crucifying the Passions in order to progress toward the Tree of Life and immortality. In short, the Virtues are viewed as the remedy of the Passions. The Virtues are gifts of the Holy Spirit and are acquired only by denying oneself, which includes the Passions, and humbling oneself beneath the Cross of Christ, the Tree of Life. My original presentation claimed that it was through the Fall that the Passions entered Man. I also claimed that, in the same way as with Adam and Eve, our daily "falls" are due to our partaking of the Forbidden Tree (i.e., we fall through disobedience). One can understand that if Man were created **with** the Passions it would cause quite a dilemma for developing a project such as my retreat.

I spoke with His Eminence following the presentation and I asked him if it were indeed true that Man was created with the Passions. He said, "Yes." Briefly I told him of my Retreat project idea. He did not think that I had to run "back to the drawing board." Instead, he said (in his best English) something like: "The marriage is good, but the wedding is bad." Everyone always laughs when I tell that story, but it took me about ten years to realize that it is what we mean by "passion" that directs our understanding. If we are simply speaking of "desire," that's one thing. If we mean sinful desires, that's another. Certainly Adam's free will included desire, longing – which fell in the Fall.[9] The "problem" of whether Man was created with the Passions, and they fell; or Man was created without the Passions, and they are the result of the Fall will be addressed in the first section of the book.

---

[9] See the note for the Appetitive Aspect of the soul in the chapter entitled "One Rule, Two Trees."

In the Church's hymns, theology, and soteriology, references to the Two Trees, Two Adams, and Two Eves are everywhere present and inescapable. You cannot attend a full cycle of services, within the period of one day, and not hear about the transgression of our first parents and the salvation wrought through the New Eve and her Son, Christ our God. The reader will also appreciate that, essentially – for them and us – there's only one rule.

As noted during the Two Trees Retreats, the subject of this book has nothing whatsoever to do with the Theory of Evolution; neither is it about so-called Creationism. Rather, it concerns the story of Adam and Eve, Jesus and Mary, you and me. "Big Bangs" and other scientific theories are stimulating topics, yet they merit only a caveat in a work concerning spiritual warfare. And, though the book has much to say concerning the Passions, it is not about The Passion of the Christ – at least as that term is popularly understood.

The number *seven* reflects not only the sum total of: *One* Rule, *Two* Trees, *Two* Adams and *Two* Eves; but also the Passions, commonly called the *Seven Deadly Sins*.[10] An easy way to remember the most common

---

[10] "While there are several noteworthy lists of sins in the Bible (e.g., Gal. 5:19-21) and while seven is a number of special significance, the Bible is not the direct source of the traditional list of vices. The individual sins that compose the catalogue of seven all occur in the Bible, however, and medieval exegetes found it relatively easy to provide scriptural warrant for the list. That pride, e.g., eventually asserted itself as the primary sin is related exegetically to Ecclus. 10:13 ('Pride is the beginning of all sin'). Figurative interpretations of such passages as Luke 8:2, concerning the exorcism of seven devils from Mary Magdalene, were used to make the Bible support the seven-sin scheme.

Passions is by using the acronym **PALE GAS**: Pride, Anger, Lust, Envy, Gluttony, Avarice, and Sloth. The book will also review their corresponding Virtues. Since there is no suitable acronym for the Virtues, readers must think of the antonyms (opposites) of the Passions. This seems fitting, as we often seem to remember the wounds more than the salve! It is a struggle to attain Virtue and, by contrast, quite easy to fall into sin. We must therefore use wise judgment and discernment in our Christian pilgrimage toward the Kingdom. It is a struggle; there is no easy path. In any case, the corresponding Virtues for the purpose of this book are: Humility, Patience, Chastity, Contentedness, Temperance, Liberality, and Diligence. Other subjects addressed in the book include: obedience, the will, spiritual warfare, and Confession.

We live in a time when there exists system upon system within Christian theology and doctrine. For those seeking a traditional understanding of the Fall, Spiritual Warfare, and Salvation, it is my hope that the Two Trees model, coupled with the analogy of the Second Adam/Second Eve, may serve as an effective tool. Yet, our tools are completely ineffective without God's saving

---

"A precursor of the Christian classification of the sins appears in the pseudepigraphal Testament of the Twelve Patriarchs, but the first Christian writer to treat the concept directly is Evagrius of Pontus, who, in his treatise *On the Eight Evil Thoughts*, expresses a theme common in the 4th-century monastic communities of the Egyptian desert: the cardinal sins involve temptations that specifically beset the ascetic life. Evagrius notes eight sins. He may, nonetheless, have been influenced by Origen's view that Joshua's destruction of seven Canaanite nations (Deut. 7:1-2) is an allegory of the soul's effort to expel sins." [David Lyle Jeffrey, *A Dictionary of Biblical Tradition in English Literature* (Grand Rapids: Eerdmans, 1992), p. 698.]

Grace. There is no way that this short book could effectively do justice to the traditional understanding of Grace – energies and essence – as revealed to us in Scripture and the Fathers. However, I have included a brief and simple note on Grace in the Appendices.

Part Two of the book includes Meditations used during Lenten workshops and retreats. In Orthodox Church Tradition, the *Great Prayer of St Ephraim the Syrian* is recited corporately during the season of Great Lent – and at other times of prayer by the pious. An exposition of that Prayer is fittingly included among the other meditations in hopes of helping to prepare the faithful for Confession. In addition, brief treatments of a short story, *The Peeler*, by Flannery O'Conner, coupled with portions of the poem, *The Hound of Heaven*, by Francis Thompson, are mingled within a framework of addiction recovery as a piece befitting the subject matter at hand.

The final three presentations – *Andrew*, *The Wait*, and *The Two Trees* – are the three main Meditations used for the Two Trees Lenten retreats. All are offered here for public or private use. The objective is repentance; the ultimate goal is salvation.

Pale Gas, the Flip Side of Virtue

And the LORD God planted a garden in Eden, in the east; and there he put the man whom he had formed. And out of the ground the LORD God made to grow every tree that is pleasant to the sight and good for food, the tree of life also in the midst of the garden, and the tree of the knowledge of good and evil. (Gen. 2:8-9)

The LORD God took the man and put him in the Garden of Eden to till it and keep it. And the LORD God commanded the man, saying, "You may freely eat of every tree of the garden; but of the tree of the knowledge of good and evil you shall not eat, for in the day that you eat of it you shall die." (Gen. 2:15-16)

Now the serpent was more subtle than any other wild creature that the LORD God had made. He said to the woman, "Did God say, 'You shall not eat of any tree of the garden'?"

And the woman said to the serpent, "We may eat of the fruit of the trees of the garden; but God said, 'You shall not eat of the fruit of the tree which is in the midst of the garden, neither shall you touch it, lest you die.'"

But the serpent said to the woman, "You will not die. For God knows that when you eat of it your eyes will be opened, and you will be like God, knowing good and evil."

So when the woman saw that the tree was good for food, and that it was a delight to the eyes, and that the tree was to be desired to make one wise, she took of its fruit and ate; and she also gave some to her husband, and he ate. (Gen. 3:1-6)

The Lord said not to eat of the Tree, but Eve thought it looked good. And the serpent said, "Oh! Did

He tell you … did He tell you it was … bad? That you would die? No! It'll make you like gods. You'll be like me." In a twisted sort of way, he was stating a fact. But, what he told her was a lie; because we know from the witness of the Church that she and Adam were deceived and the devil is a liar.

Eve and Adam ate from the tree of the knowledge of good and evil. Eve, who was created as a 'help-meet' for Adam, was beguiled by the adversary and instead of helping Adam, harmed him. Through her disobedience, Eve – "the mother of the living" – bore the "fruit of death" to Adam and all mankind.

> For as in Adam all die, so also in Christ shall all be made alive … Thus it is written, "The first man Adam became a living being"; the last Adam became a life-giving spirit. But it is not the spiritual which is first but the physical, and then the spiritual. The first man was from the earth, a man of dust; the second man is from heaven. As was the man of dust, so are those who are of the dust; and as is the man of heaven, so are those who are of heaven. Just as we have borne the image of the man of dust, we shall also bear the image of the man of heaven. (1 Cor. 15:22, 45-49)

As we shall see, Mary, the Theotokos, through her obedience, bore the fruit of Life to all mankind: Christ, the New Man, the Second Adam. The Virgin Mary is in the Church as the 'Second Eve'. If you will, Our Lord and His mother serve as the "flip side" of our first parents,

Adam and Eve. Such is also the case with the Passions and Virtues. And, as we shall see, this flip side can also be seen in the commands: "Do not eat" and "Take, eat."

For the purposes of this project, we need to visualize the Two Trees and their fruit. On the Tree of the Knowledge of Good and Evil we have the Passions; on the Tree of Life, the Virtues. In the sketch of this vision,[11] there are two trees represented, both set upon a hill, with a valley in between which is labeled "wilderness."[12] The tree on the hill, to the left, is fruitful and set in a grassy garden; the one on the right depicts the crucifixion upon a barren hill. Although an image of the sun appears above the tree in the garden, it is labeled "night." The other tree on a hill, the Cross, is covered by a dark cloud labeled "day." Several other words and phrases describe the tree on the left: "Satan, sin, and death," "clothed as royalty," and "damnation." The words and phrases which describe the tree on the right are: "faith, hope, and charity."[13] "naked with a cross," and "salvation." Things are not as they seem; they are all flipped around from one's expectations.

Beneath the tree in the garden are listed the Passions: Pride, Anger, Lust, Envy, Gluttony, Avarice, and Sloth. There is also a symbol for the Decalogue ("X"), or Ten Commandments, with a slash mark through it which indicates that the Commandments are disobeyed in this garden. Also listed under the tree in the garden are various ways by which we sin: counsel, command, consent,

---

[11] See Appendix I.

[12] Oftentimes the season of Great Lent is compared to a wilderness in our journey toward the celebration of the Christian Passover (Pascha/Easter).

[13] Upson, p. 32.

provocation, praise/flattery, concealment, partaking, silence, and defense of the sin committed.[14]

Across the wilderness, beneath the image of the tree on the hill, we find listed the Seven Capital Virtues: Humility, Mildness, Chastity, Happiness, Temperance, Liberality, and Diligence. Beneath the Cross is a list of the gifts of the Holy Spirit – wisdom, understanding, counsel, fortitude, knowledge, piety, fear of God and a list of the fruits of the Holy Spirit; love, joy, peace, patience, kindness, goodness, long-suffering, mildness, fidelity, modesty, continence, chastity.[15] Finally, under the tree on the hill, there is a symbol ("X") which indicates that obedience to the commands of God in the Decalogue is the rule.

In Greek, the word **Passion** signifies literally that which happens to a person or thing, an experience undergone passively; hence an appetite or impute such as anger, desire, or jealousy, which violently dominates the soul. Many Greek Fathers regard the Passions as something intrinsically evil, a "disease" of the soul.

While some Fathers (e.g. St. John Climacus) include the sin of Vainglory[16], most lists of the Passions include what are sometimes referred to as the Cardinal Sins: Pride, Anger, Lust, Envy, Gluttony, Avarice, Sloth. Each letter in the acronym PALE GAS may be used to identify one of the Passions, commonly known as the Seven Deadly Sins.

---

[14] Upson, pp. 29-30.
[15] Upson, pp. 29-30.
[16] **VAINGLORY:** extreme self-pride and boastfulness; excessive and ostentatious vanity. *Webster's New Universal Unabridged Dictionary* (London: Dorset & Baber, 1979).

P – pride
A – anger
L – lust
E - envy
G – gluttony
A – avarice (greed)
S – sloth

Unfortunately, for ease of memory, there is no handy acronym for the Virtues. However, they are the opposites – the flip side – of the listed Passions:

Pride – Humility
Anger – Patience
Lust – Chastity
Envy – Contentment
Gluttony - Moderation
Avarice – Liberality
Sloth – Diligence

In our fallen state, we have more experience with the Passions than with the Virtues. The names of the Seven Deadlies come to mind much easier than their antidotes, the Virtues. This, in a way, seems fitting as the acquisition of Virtue requires great struggle. "Even Adam, who was in a blissful state of communion with God in Paradise, lost it all because he did not struggle."[17]

In the illustration,[18] the tree of the knowledge of good and evil, in truth, offers only death. But it looks most

---

[17] Hierotheos Vlachos, *A Night in the Desert of the Holy Mountain*, trans. Effie Mavromichali (Greece: Birth of the Theotokos Monastery, 1991) p. 61.
[18] Appendix I.

inviting because if you only have a choice between these two, the one with the dead man hanging on it certainly doesn't look to be a tree of life. We can move toward the garden we're familiar with, the one with PALE GAS, which always looks inviting. (It's not as if we sin once, regret it, and never go back!) The forbidden tree presents itself as being easy, comforting, and good. We can justify this, can't we? The Cross always looks hard. No matter how many times you've made professions of faith, turned your life around, gone to confession/communion, or read the Scriptures – the Cross never looks easy. This moment of choice, longing for the Cross but looking toward the forbidden, is where all too often we find ourselves.

Sometimes we struggle over a certain sin, perhaps one of habit, and we figure out a way to justify it. It's like being on a diet to lose weight and, upon losing a few pounds, going out to eat to celebrate. "I've been so good lately; it wouldn't hurt if I was bad just a wee bit!" Like Eve before us, we're drawn to the forbidden tree because it looks inviting. It seems surrounded by perpetual day, but in truth it's always dark. The Cross, which looks so foreboding, in truth is surrounded by light – which brings light to our life. But, of course, this tree always involves death – the death of the man who hangs on the tree and our own. Beneath that Tree, we must die to self, over and over. With the forbidden tree, we allow ourselves to be deceived by the serpent over and over again.

The forbidden tree promises life, but always leads to death. The other tree, which presents death, is the only way to true life. Part of the problem is we're not tempted by Virtue. The Passions are another story. The Virtues belong to God. When we participate in Virtue, we participate in the life of God. As with marriage, where one keeps the covenant with husband or wife because of love, we participate in Virtue because we love God. We dally with the Passions because we love ourselves.

As with our first parents, we are deceived. This is one of the reasons we should not seek visions in our prayers. We shouldn't ask God to show us great signs. The devil also knows what we desire. Once you make your will known – he's a deceiver – he can only imitate God: Truth comes first, then deception. What's the most popular or best working disguise the devil has? Right: he's an angel of light. He is deceitful and everything he does, in truth, only brings darkness. The Enemy hates God and being unable to fight Him directly he fights against us – who are in God's image.

God is love. Love always creates. Love – *God* – can't help but create! Love never tears down; love never destroys; love is never dark. The deceiver can only bring a shadow of the good which, as is the nature of shadow, consists of darkness. The opposite of creation is nothing. God created out of nothing. Evil is **no** *thing*. It is the eternal descent toward nothing.

Yet, though we may know these things, we find ourselves falling over and over again into the same trap, the same deception. Like the classic definition of madness, we do the same thing, day in and day out, expecting different results. In other words, though we've tasted the bitter fruit time and again, we continually search for life on the forbidden tree … which always leads to death.

Fr Joseph David Huneycutt

THE FALL

So when the woman saw that the tree was good for food, and that it was a delight to the eyes, and that the tree was to be desired to make one wise, she took of its fruit and ate; and she also gave some to her husband, and he ate.

Then the eyes of both were opened, and they knew that they were naked; and they sewed fig leaves together and made themselves aprons. And they heard the sound of the LORD God walking in the garden in the cool of the day, and the man and his wife hid themselves from the presence of the LORD God among the trees of the garden.

But the LORD God called to the man, and said to him, "Where are you?"

And he said, "I heard the sound of thee in the garden, and I was afraid, because I was naked; and I hid myself."

He said, "Who told you that you were naked? Have you eaten of the tree of which I commanded you not to eat?"

The man said, "The woman whom thou gavest to be with me, she gave me fruit of the tree, and I ate."

Then the LORD God said to the woman, "What is this that you have done?" The woman said, "The serpent beguiled me, and I ate."

The LORD God said to the serpent, "Because you have done this, cursed are you above all cattle, and above all wild animals; upon your belly you shall go, and dust you shall eat all the days of your life. I will put enmity between you and the woman, and between your seed and her seed; he shall bruise your head, and you shall bruise his heel."

To the woman he said, "I will greatly multiply your pain in childbearing; in pain you shall bring forth children, yet your desire shall be for your husband, and he shall rule over you."

And to Adam he said, "Because you have listened to the voice of your wife, and have eaten of the tree of which I commanded you, 'You shall not eat of it,' cursed is the ground because of you; in toil you shall eat of it all the days of your life; thorns and thistles it shall bring forth to you; and you shall eat the plants of the field. In the sweat of your face you shall eat bread till you return to the ground, for out of it you were taken; you are dust, and to dust you shall return."

The man called his wife's name Eve, because she was the mother of all living. And the LORD God made for Adam and for his wife garments of skins [[19]], and clothed them.

Then the LORD God said, "Behold, the man has become like one of us, knowing good and evil; and now, lest he put forth his hand and take also of the tree of life, and eat, and live for ever" – therefore the LORD God sent him forth from the garden of Eden, to till the ground from which he was taken.

He drove out the man; and at the east of the Garden of Eden he placed the cherubim, and a flaming sword which turned every way, to guard the way to the tree of life. (Gen. 6:3-24)

---

[19] For a thorough and patristic treatment of the "garments of skin," please see Panayiotis Nellas, *Deification in Christ – Orthodox Perspectives on the Nature of the Human Person*, trans. Norman Russell (Crestwood, New York: St. Vladimir's Seminary Press, 1997).

Angels and Men, You and Me

We, you and I, know that we are vexed by the Passions. Why? Prior to the Fall of Adam and Eve is the Fall of Lucifer and some of the angels. What transpired to lead to the Fall of the Archangel Lucifer (Satan, the Enemy, the Adversary, etc.) and his hosts? Does the Fall of the Angels hold clues as to whether the Passions are part of creation, or a result of the Fall? Is the same answer perpetual within the daily falls of man? Realizing that we must speak in metaphors of great mysteries – and that there is no one single and easy answer provided by the Fathers and the Tradition of the Church – these questions will be surveyed and addressed in this chapter.

> If with the Lord's help you cleanse your heart and uproot sin – struggling for the knowledge that is more divine and see in your intellect things invisible to most people – you must not on this account be arrogant towards anyone. For an angel, being incorporeal is more pure and full of spiritual knowledge than any other created thing; yet it was an angel who, in exalting himself, fell like lightning from heaven. Thus his pride was reckoned by God as impurity.[20]

An often heard quick answer to the question of the Fall is Pride. "Pride goeth before a fall." Empirically, this rings true. Yet, we should not base the fundamentals of the Faith on experience. What is more fundamental to

---

[20] St Philotheos of Sinai, PV3, p.19.

the human condition – and the remedy of faith in Christ
Jesus – than the Fall? Yet, human experience is post-Fall
(postlapsarian). How can one possibly begin with one's
experience in examining this question? In so doing, one
deceives himself all the more. One's experience is also
fallen. Instead, one must begin with the adversary, Satan,
and those who fell with him.

> How are you fallen from heaven, O
> Lucifer, Day Star, son of Dawn (Is.
> 14:12a)!

> And the angels which did not keep their
> own position but left their proper
> dwelling have been kept by him in eternal
> chains in the nether gloom until the
> judgment of the great day (Jude 6).

Pride, as we know and generally experience it, is
inherently bad. So how is it that, prior to eating of the
fruit of the Forbidden Tree, Man succumbed to the sin of
pride? Or, how is it that the angelic powers fell prey to
something greater than themselves? In other words, how
could they become subject to something which is contrary
to their Creator? Metropolitan Hierotheos Vlachos writes:

> In church we often speak of the fall of
> man and the death which came as a result
> of the fall. Spiritual death came first, and
> bodily death followed. The soul lost the
> uncreated grace of God, the nous[21] ceased

---

[21] **NOUS:** The word has various uses in Patristic teaching. It
indicates either the soul or the heart or even an energy of the
soul. Yet, the nous is mainly the eye of the soul; the purest part

to have a relationship with God and was darkened. It transmitted this darkening and dying to the body. According to Gregory of Sinai, man's body was created incorruptible and 'such it will be resurrected,' and the soul was created dispassionate. Since there was a very tenacious link between soul and body because of their interpenetration and communication, both were corrupted. 'The soul acquired the qualities of passions, or rather demons, and the body became like irrational beasts due to the condition into which it fell and the prevalence of corruption.' Since the soul and the body were corrupted, they formed 'one animal being, unreasoning and senseless, subject to anger and lust.' This is how, according to Scripture, man became 'joined to the beasts and like them.' Through the fall, man's soul filled with passions, his body became like the beasts. Man wore the skin garments of decay and mortality and became like irrational animals.[22]

---

of the soul; the highest attention. It is also called noetic energy and it is not identified with reason (Hierotheos Vlachos, *The Illness and Cure of the Soul in the Orthodox Tradition*, trans. Effie Mavromichali (Greece: Birth of the Theotokos Monastery, 1993), p. 40).

[22] Hierotheos Vlachos, *Orthodox Psychotherapy - The Science of the Fathers*, trans. Esther Williams (Greece: Birth of the Theotokos Monastery, 1994), p. 112.

Pride is one of the Passions. If Man were created with the Passions, if they did not enter the world with the Fall; if, until the Fall (when Man's nous was darkened), the passions were essentially good, how is it that Adam and Eve fell by pride – when pride itself was yet to fall? For example, St Gregory of Sinai says that "thoughts are the words of demons and the forerunners of the passions. First comes the thought, and then the sin is committed."[23] Thus it seems that something must precede the Passions. One might label this as presumption, but this judgment can only be made, in my opinion, postlapsarian! Again, St Peter of Damascus: "For since Adam's transgression we are all subject to the passions because of our constant association with them."[24]

> Moreover, the angels and all the radiant and divine powers practice and preserve this virtue [humility], knowing how Satan fell when he became proud, and how he lies in the abyss as a fearful warning of such a fall to both angels and men. Through his pride he proved himself in God's sight more degraded than any other created thing. We also know that Adam fell through pride.[25]

However, pride is not the only cause mentioned in Scripture and the Fathers. There are other reasons given for the great demise – such as envy:

---

[23] OP, p. 218.
[24] PV3, p. 77.
[25] PV3, p. 20.

For God created man for incorruption,
and made him in the image of his eternity,
but through the devil's envy death entered
the world, and those who belong to this
party experience it (Wis. 2:23, 24).

What was it that caused Lucifer's envy? St
Gregory of Nyssa speaks of the envy of God, while
Anselm of Canterbury speaks of the envy of Man;
regarding the latter, the devil was envious of Adam
because he was created in the image of God and had
control of all creation.

Others, as mentioned above, view the sin of
presumption as the cause of the Fall. According to St
Makarios of Egypt:

Presumption is an abomination to the
Lord, and it was this that originally
expelled man from paradise when he
heard the serpent say, 'You will be like
gods' (Gen. 3:5), and put his trust in this
vain hope.[26]

Adding to this, St Peter of Damascus says:

For a person derives no benefit from the
other virtues, even though he dwells in
heaven, if he is in the grip of the
presumption that led to the fall of the
devil, Adam and many others.[27]

---

[26] PV3, p. 323.
[27] PV3, p. 271.

I do not say, however, that Satan's fall was essentially because of pride, envy, or presumption. Rather, I submit that, as in the fall of Man – even in our daily falls – the catalyst is the disobedient will.[28] The **will** is active first. **Pride** is the first fruit of a disobedient will.

> If you will understand what kind of sin the devil committed, and what kind Adam committed, you will find nothing else but pride alone. But the devil and Adam became proud by reason of the great glory which they were vouchsafed in abundance. Being clothed with glory, not after humility and disgrace – for this reason they became proud. They had never seen humility and did not know what this humility and disgrace might be which follow when one is thrown down from the heights of glory; therefore, not having the fear which comes from this happening, they became proud. Just think, then, how great was the humility of the Lord Jesus when He, being God, humbled Himself even to voluntary death and died on the Cross a death which served as punishment for the worst kind of people. And thus, there was one sin, pride, and one virtue, great humility.[29]

---

[28] Labeling the Fall, or "falls," with titles of "pride," "envy," or "presumption" is, in my opinion, postlapsarian. It is a judgment. First comes the will.

[29] St. Symeon the New Theologian, *The First-Created Man: Seven Homilies by St. Symeon the New Theologian*, trans. Seraphim Rose (Platina, California: Saint Herman Press, 1994), p. 68.

One Rule, Two Trees

> *Then as one man's trespass led to condemnation for all men, so one man's act of righteousness leads to acquittal and life for all men. For as by one man's disobedience many were made sinners, so by one man's obedience many will be made righteous. Law came in, to increase the trespass; but where sin increased, grace abounded all the more, so that, as sin reigned in death, grace also might reign through righteousness to eternal life through Jesus Christ our Lord (Rom. 5:18-21).*

After the transgression in the Garden of Eden, we no longer hear of the Tree of Life. What happened to it? St Ephraim the Syrian says that it was subsumed into the earth only to sprout again on Calvary. With that analogy in mind, what hangs on this Tree of Life according to the teaching of the Church? Life itself! Christ.

We all know the story; in the Garden of Eden there were Two Trees and One Rule: "Don't eat of this tree." But, from what has been said above, and from our own experience, we are obviously not very good at obedience. Lucifer, Adam, and all of mankind were, are, and continue to be disobedient. Adam was called to obedience. Given all of Paradise and Communion with God, Adam was given but one command:

> The Lord God took the man and put him in the Garden of Eden to till it and keep it. And the Lord God commanded the man, saying, "You may freely eat of every tree of the garden; but of the tree of the knowledge of good and evil you shall not eat, for in the day that you eat of it you shall die" (Gen. 2:15-17).

27

By now, everyone knows of Adam's *dis*-obedience. He transgressed the law of God. Instead of heeding the words of his Creator, Adam did the opposite. St Makarios of Egypt expounds on what such disobedience affects, saying:

> Those who have withdrawn from the world and lead a godly and devout life are still in many cases subject to the veil of the passions to which we all became liable through Adam's transgression: I refer to the carnal will, fittingly called death by St Paul when he said that the 'will of the flesh is death' (Rom. 8:6).[30]

St Gregory of Sinai, continuing this theme, says:

> When by His life-giving breath God created the intelligent and noetic soul, "He did not make it have rage and animal lust; He endowed the soul only with the appetitive power and with the courage to be lovingly attracted."[31] With the creation

---

[30] PV3, p. 349.

[31] Appetitive Aspect of the Soul, or the soul's desiring power: one of the three aspects or powers of the soul according to the tripartite division formulated by Plato and on the whole accepted by the Greek Christian Fathers. The other two are, first, the intelligent aspect or power; and the second, the incensive aspect or power, which often manifests itself as wrath or anger, but which can be more generally defined as the force provoking vehement feelings. The three aspects or powers can be used positively, in accordance with nature and created by God, or

of the soul "neither lust nor anger was included in its being." These came as a result of sin.[32]

Truth comes first, then deception. And, as St John Climacus states: "It is impossible that the devil should act contrary to his own will."[33] In other words, in his (current) envy toward the Good, the Adversary can only imitate. Yet, his imitation is one of darkness instead of light. In discussing angels, St Peter of Damascus writes:

> Even the devil, having lost the knowledge of God, and so inevitably becoming ignorant in his ingratitude and pride, cannot of himself know what to do. On the contrary, he sees what God does to save us and maliciously learns from this and contrives similar things for our destruction. For he hates God and, being unable to fight Him directly, he fights against us who are in God's image, thinking to avenge himself on God in this way; and, as St John Chrysostom says, he finds us obedient to his will. For instance, he sees how God created Eve as a helpmate for Adam, and so enlists her co-operation to bring about disobedience

---

negatively, in a way contrary to nature and leading to sin. For instance, the incensive power can be used positively to repel demonic attacks or to intensify desire for God; but when not controlled, it can also lead to self-indulgent, disruptive thought and action (PV3, p. 356).

[32] OP, pp. 107-108.

[33] LDA, 4:109, p. 48.

and transgression. Or, again, God gave a commandment so that by keeping it Adam might be mindful of the great gifts he had received and thank his Benefactor for them; but the devil made of this commandment the starting point of disobedience and death.[34]

Peter of Damaskos goes on to state:

> Instead of prophets, he [Satan] promotes false prophets; instead of apostles, false apostles; instead of law, lawlessness; instead of virtue, vice; instead of commandments, transgression; instead of righteousness, foul heresies.[35]

Man's — and Satan's — first transgression was one of a disobedient will. True, we humans are deceived, but only when we first rebel against the will of God. Then the deceiver takes full advantage of our misdirected submission.

> Evil entered the world through the will. It is not a nature, but a condition. According to St Gregory of Nyssa, sin is a disease of the will which is deceived, and takes a mere shadow of the good for the good itself.[36]

---

[34] PV3, pp. 80-81.
[35] PV3, pp. 80-81.
[36] Vladimir Lossky, *The Mystical Theology of the Eastern Church* (Crestwood, New York: St Vladimir's Seminary Press, 1976), p. 128.

Perhaps the "shadow of the good" of which St Gregory speaks is a reference to the falling of the Passions. If man were indeed created with the Passions – they fell through his disobedience. It was the disobedience that came first. Lossky continues:

> For this reason, the very desire to taste of the fruit of the knowledge of good and evil was itself a sin, for, according to St Gregory, knowledge presupposes a certain disposition towards the object one wishes to know, and evil, being itself non-existent, ought not to be known. Evil becomes a reality only by means of the will, in which alone it subsists. It is the will which gives evil a certain being.[37]

Thus, the disobedient will is the "first cause" of the Fall of both Lucifer and Adam. Postlapsarian Man is now subject to the Passions; the nous is darkened. It was through the spirit world that the first Fall occurred. Yet, it was only **_after_** this fall, the Fall of Lucifer and other angels, that Man is led to corruption of his own spirit – due to a disobedient will. Vladimir Lossky writes:

> Before entering the earthly world through Adam's will, evil already had its beginnings in the spiritual world. It was the will of the angelic spirits, eternally fixed in their enmity to God, which first gave birth to evil. And evil is nothing

---

[37] MT, p. 128.

other than an attraction of the will towards nothing, a negation of being, of creation, and above all of God, a furious hatred of grace against which the **rebellious will** puts up an implacable resistance. Even though they have become spirits of darkness, the fallen angels remain creatures of God, and their rejection of God represents a despairing intercourse with the nothingness which they will never find. Their eternal descent towards nothing will have no end.[38]

In their descent, the wicked spirits try to ensnare Man to drag him down with them. This would not be possible, had Man not been disobedient to God's command. Yet, since the Fall, the adversarial spirits make war against Man by use of the Passions (which have tainted Man's spirit). Concerning the adversarial spirits, the demons, St Seraphim of Sarov states:

They are hideous; their conscious rejection of divine grace has transformed them into angels of darkness, and unimaginable horrors. Being angelic creatures, they possess enormous strength. The least among them could destroy the earth, did not divine grace render their hatred of God's creation powerless. Therefore they seek to destroy

---

[38] MT, p. 129; emphasis mine.

creation from within, by turning human freedom towards evil.[39]

St Peter of Damaskos adds:

> Because of the great obscurity produced by the passions, a person may become so demented as to imagine in his lack of humility that he is the equal of the angels, or even greater than they. It was precisely this lack of humility on Lucifer's part that was enough without any other sin to turn him into darkness. What, then, will be the fate of a man who is without humility, since he is but dust and mortal, not to say a sinner? Perhaps in his blindness he does not believe that he has sinned. St John Chrysostom says that the perfect man will certainly become the equal of the angels, as the Lord affirms; but he will do so in the resurrection of the dead, and not in this present world. Even then the perfect will not be angels, but 'equal to the angels' (Luke 20:36). This means that men cannot forsake their own nature, though like the angels they can become changeless through grace and released from all necessity, free in everything they do, possessing ceaseless joy, love of God, and all that 'the eye has not seen, and the ear has not heard' (1 Cor. 2:9).[40]

---

[39] MT, p. 129.
[40] PV3, p. 177.

The rebellion is in the will. Pride is a fruit of a submissive will that has rebelled against the will of God and submitted itself to Satan, sin, and death. What we call the *Passions* can be viewed as *Judgments*. It is usually only after the fact when we are able to label our sins with names. First, we transgress the will of God by our disobedience. We choose to do that which is contrary to God's commandments. Again, quoting Lossky:

> The commandment of God marks out for the human will the way which leads to deification, the way of detachment from all that is not God. Human will has chosen the opposite way, has become separated from God and has submitted to the tyranny of the devil.[41]

One falls into this habitual trap of the "opposite way" time and again. This is the struggle of which St Paul speaks in his Epistle to the Romans: "I do not understand my own actions. For I do not do what I want, but I do the very thing I hate" (7:15). This continual transgression of God's commandments leads, of course, to death.

Following his disobedience, Adam blamed the woman, and the woman blamed the snake. Lossky expands:

> Man sinned freely. But what constitutes original sin? The Fathers distinguish many moments in this decision of free will which separates man from God. The

---

[41] MT, p. 130.

moral, and therefore personal, moment is for all of them, to be found in the disobedience to and transgression of the divine commandment. If man had received the commandment in a spirit of filial love, he would have responded to the will of God with a complete sacrifice; he would detach himself willingly, not only from the forbidden fruit, but from every external object, in order to live only for God, to aspire solely to union with Him. The commandment of God marks out for the human will the way which leads to deification, the way of detachment from all that is not God. Human will has chosen the opposite way, has become separated from God and has submitted to the tyranny of the devil. St Gregory of Nyssa, and St Maximos, pay special attention to the natural aspect of sin. Instead of following its natural disposition towards God, the human spirit has turned towards the world; instead of spiritualizing the body it has itself entered into the stream of animal and sensory life, and become subject to the material conditions. St Symeon the New Theologian sees a progressive development of sin in the fact that man, instead of repenting, tries to justify himself before God. Adam declines all responsibility for Eve, 'the woman whom thou gavest to be with me', and so makes God the root cause of his fall. Eve accuses the serpent. In this refusal to recognize that the unique origin of evil is in their own free will, men reject the possibility of freeing themselves from evil and submit their freedoms to external necessity. The will hardens, and shuts itself off from God. 'Man has closed up within himself the springs of divine grace,' says Philaret of Moscow.[42]

In some respects it seems that the question of whether Man was created **with** the Passions or whether they are the result of the Fall is trivial, an "apples and oranges" question. However, one thing is certain: fallen humanity is continually involved in spiritual warfare against the Passions. Yet, here still, the **_will_** comes first. We tend to "label" our sin only after the fact. St Gregory of Nyssa writes:

> For the Creator would himself be the author of sins if the compulsion to transgress emanated from the passions. It is the use that our free will makes of them that determines the fault.[43]

It is precisely because of this spiritual warfare that Mankind is in need of a Savior. And, it is in doing battle within ourselves and the Passions that we fight the good fight of faith. Again, St Makarios of Egypt:

---

[42] MT, pp. 130-131.

[43] Hans Urs von Balthasar, *Presence and Thought - An Essay on the Religious Philosophy of Gregory of Nyssa* (San Francisco: Ignatius Press, 1995), p. 75.

In accordance with divine providence, the
devil was not sent at once to the Gehenna
assigned to him, but his sentence was
postponed in order to let him test and try
man's free will. In this way, he
unintentionally fosters greater maturity
and righteousness in the saints by
promoting their patient endurance, and so
is the cause of their greater glory; and, at
the same time, through his malevolence
and his scheming against the saints he
justifies more fully his own punishment.[44]

Perhaps one can split hairs and claim that the
Passions were inherent in Adam and it was only at the Fall
that they were implanted in the soul. Yet such a division
of soul and body is contrary to Orthodox teaching. St
Isaac of Syria, in his work, *Spiritual Training*, says:

By nature the soul is without sinful
passion. Passions are something added to
the soul by its fault ... The natural state
of the soul is luminous and pure through
absorbing the divine light ... The state
contrary to nature ... is found in
passionate men who serve the passions.
When you hear that it is necessary to
withdraw from the world ... to purify
yourself from what is of the world, you
must understand the term *world*. "World"
is a collective name embracing what are
called passions. When we speak of

---

[44] PV3, p. 299.

passions collectively, we call them the world ... the world is carnal life and a minding of flesh.[45]

Yes! It is precisely because Adam chooses to obey creation instead of the Creator – the world vs. the Lord – that he, and all mankind, falls. Adam longed for the glories of this world so much that he lost the glory with which he was created. He listened to a creature instead of the Creator. And, does this dilemma not still plague his descendants? St Gregory of Nyssa writes:

> Christ was like a man "who perceived a weak person carried away by a raging current. He knows that he himself will be sucked up by the whirlpool, wounded and lacerated by the rocks, swept away by the water. But pity for this man in danger stimulates him. He does not hesitate to throw himself into the current." He enters, therefore, without reservations into the flow of duration. But in order to save the one who is drowning, he must "jump" *from on high*, that is to say, he must bring us the integrity of our own nature. It is very much a necessity that he not be born of a mortal man who is subject to the "passions" but that he bring us that nature that is *antecedent* to the "passions"

---

[45] Hopko, Thomas, quoted in *An Elementary Handbook on the Orthodox Faith,* Volume 4: Spirituality (New York: The Department of Religious Education, The Orthodox Church in America, 1976), p. 22.

(which, indeed, as we know, are linked in a mysterious way to sin).[46]

There it is: "the nature that is antecedent to the 'passions'." The only way that we can struggle toward this nature which humanity once possessed – that is, ***potential*** toward perfection – is through Him who is the Life.

This struggle of spiritual warfare involves the slaying of the Passions – which keep us attached to this world – and the acquisition of the Virtues. As Adam was created potentially perfect, we are only perfected by grace through the Second Adam, the God-Man, Christ. And, as should be abundantly clear, the greatest struggle is that of ***obedience***. For without obedience we are fallen. Yet, through our obedience to Christ and His Church, we may be saved.

> And Mary said, "Behold, I am the handmaid of the Lord; let it be to me according to your word." And the angel departed from her. (Lk. 1:38).

This salvific remedy is the opposite of the disobedient transgression in the Garden of Eden. Both Eve and Mary were greeted with the words of an Archangel. The former fell through uniting her will with that of a deceptive creature; the latter is praised by all generations due to her uniting her will with that of the Creator.

Therefore, within the tradition of the Church regarding the Second Adam and the Second Eve can be found the same understanding with regard to the Two

---

[46] P&T, pp. 135-136.

Trees. We must, by our will – in cooperation with God's will and grace – be led from disobedience to obedience; from the Passions to the Virtues; and, through the Sacrament of Repentance, from the Tree of Death to the Tree of Life.

> Inasmuch, therefore, as the Cross has become as it were the altar of this fearful sacrifice – for on the Cross the Son of God died for the fall of man – therefore the Cross is justly revered and worshipped and depicted as the sign of common resurrection of all men, so that those who bow down before the wood of the Cross might be delivered from the curse of Adam and receive the blessing and grace of God for the doing of every virtue.[47]

---

[47] TFCM, p. 48.

Two Adams, Two Eves

Having rivaled the first-created Adam by my transgressions, I realize that I am stripped naked of God and of the everlasting kingdom and bliss through my sins.

Alas, wretched soul! Why are you like the first Eve? For you have wickedly looked and been bitterly wounded, and you have touched the tree and rashly tasted the forbidden food.

The place of bodily Eve has been taken for me by the Eve of my mind in the shape of a passionate thought in the flesh, showing me sweet things, yet ever making me taste and swallow bitter things.

Adam was rightly exiled from Eden for not keeping Thy one commandment, O Savior. But what shall I suffer who am always rejecting Thy living words? [48]

Yet the connection between sin and exile is often denied. A counselor at a rescue mission once told of the intake interviews wherein each man was asked about his history. The stories, with little variation, involved mostly drinking and drugging, coupled with promiscuity. The question was later asked: "How's your relationship with God?" Almost 100% of the interviewees answered along the lines of, "Oh! Me and God are tight! Yep. God and I are close."

> If so be that ye have heard him, and have been taught by him, as the truth is in Jesus: That ye put off concerning the

---

[48] *The Great Canon - The Work of Saint Andrew of Crete* (Jordanville, New York: Holy Trinity Monastery, 1992), pp. 5-6.

former conversation the old man, which is corrupt according to the deceitful lusts; And be renewed in the spirit of your mind; And that ye put on the new man, which after God is created in righteousness and true holiness (Eph. 4:21-24, King James Version).

It happens to all of us: our "old man" (Eph. 4:22) plays a trick on us, leading us to neglect the one thing needful. Though we long for God, we fill up our lives with that which leads us far from Him. In truth, we've only got one chore: "The thing that will move God more on the Day of Judgment is the work each one of us has done on his old man."[49]

If any of us does not recognize that he is Adam, the one who sinned before God in Paradise, how can he recognize and think that the coming down of the Son and Word of God was for him? A law was established after the Fall, that just as each of us is Adam, that is, a corruptible and mortal man, not by reason of our own sin, but by reason of the disobedience of our first ancestor Adam, from whose seed we come; so each of us is of Christ, immortal and incorrupt, not for the sake of our own virtues, but for the sake of the obedience of the second Adam, Who is Christ our Lord Who came down from

---

[49] Elder Paisios of Mount Athos, *Epistles* (Thessaloniki, Greece: Holy Monastery of Evangelist John the Theologian, 2002), p. 150.

Heaven; we become bone of His bone and flesh of His flesh. And just as corruption and death come down from generation to generation from the old Adam, so also incorruption and immortality come down to Christians from the new Adam.[50]

Just as the Passions are the opposite of the God-pleasing Virtues, one vexed by vice leaves little room for God's saving grace. For this reason, we are called to put off the old man, which is Adam, and put on the New Man, Christ. We participate in Christ by the Grace of God, the Holy Spirit.

And as it is impossible for a house to stand without a foundation, so also it is impossible for the soul which believes in Christ to manifest a God-pleasing life if in it there will not be laid as a foundation the grace of the Holy Spirit. For fasting, and vigils, and sleeping on the floor, and prostrations, and praying, and every other suffering of evil is nothing without Divine grace. And if you hear that anyone after evident Christian works has fallen away from Christ, know that at that time he was without the grace of God. For the Holy Spirit gives life to the soul, as the soul gives life to the body; and the soul becomes strong, firm, and constant.[51]

---

[50] TFCM, p. 79.
[51] TFCM, p. 71.

God created Man in His image and likeness to be in communion with Him. Man has free will to respond to this relationship. Although created in the image and after the likeness of God, he does not sustain communion with God. Though fashioned in God's image, the likeness has been lost and, through sin, the image tarnished.

> In one disastrous moment, then, God-loving Eve yielded to temptation, from the corrupter of her freedom. Satan abused her, the archangel who had become "the father of lies" (cf. Jn. 8:44), the executioner of men and the opponent of God. He whispered sweet lies into the ears of the woman. In effect, he said this to her: 'Eat of this forbidden tree, and your eyes will be opened, and you will be gods. God knows that it was for this reason forbidden you, so you will not be as He is. He cannot stand competition, He is envious.' At these words, Eve's ears buzzed, her spiritual sight was blinded, and confusion overcame her mind. She immediately confided a slander of God to the conspirator, trusting lies against the Truth, believing the murderer of man in opposition to the Lover of mankind. And in the instant when she confided in the polluted serpent with polluted lies, her soul forfeited harmony, she dismissed the chords of godly music from herself, and

love turned cold for the Creator, the God of love.[52]

The first Eve, by her disobedience, bore the fruit of death to Adam, all Mankind. The new Eve, Mary, by her obedience, bears the Fruit of Life, the new Adam, her son and God, to all mankind. This, in a nutshell, is the very heart of our Christian Faith. It represents the difference in the fruit born of disobedience and that brought forth in obedience.

> Eve, being a virgin and incorrupt, conceived the word spoken of the serpent, and brought forth disobedience and death. But Mary the Virgin answered, 'May it be according to Thy word,' and received faith and grace.[53]

Jesus, the new Adam – the "new man" – was born in the city of Bethlehem. The word "Bethlehem" means "house of bread." The new Adam was born in the House of Bread and laid in a Manger, a feeding trough. Many times in the Gospel (eight times in John Chapter 6, alone), Jesus refers to himself as bread. Traditionally, this is reflected in the hymn Orthodox priests recite as they begin the preparation of the bread for Communion:

---

[52] Joanna Manley, *The Lament of Eve* (Menlo Park, California: Monastery Books, 1993) #37, p. 82.
[53] Elder Cleopa of Romania, *The Truth of Our Faith - Discourses from Holy Scripture on the Tenets of Christian Orthodoxy*, ed. Peter Alban Heers (Thessalonica, Greece: Uncut Mountain Press, 2000), p. 86.

> Make ready, O Bethlehem, for Eden hath been opened for all. Prepare, O Ephratha, for the tree of life hath blossomed forth in the cave from the Virgin; for her womb did appear as a spiritual paradise in which is planted the divine Plant, whereof eating we shall live and not die as Adam. Christ shall be born, raising the image that fell of old.[54]

The image that fell of old is that of the old man, our forefather Adam. Our first mother, too, reflected a tarnished image.

> A face does not reflect itself in troubled waters. Neither did Eve see God in the mirror of her troubled soul. She was looking at the tree, full of mixed fruit — good and bad. Looking with her confused soul, she no longer saw God as higher than herself. She had abandoned God. God and the devil did not remain in the same regard. There was then no other woman to support her against Satan and his carnal viewpoint. And with these eyes and this new sight, she saw the forbidden fruit as good to eat, pleasant to look at and giving much knowledge. Oh, knowledge not only of good but also of evil! But the outcome of a mixture of good and evil is evil. In place of love all is

---

[54] Bishop Basil [Essey], comp., *The Liturgikon - The Book of Divine Services for the Priest and Deacon*, 2nd ed. (Englewood, New Jersey: Antakya Press, 1994), p. 245.

filled with three desires: lust for bodily pleasure, desire for possessions, and desire for knowledge. Having lost God, she had begun to look for support in things. But the emptiness, caused by draining the abandoned God from the soul, all the world cannot fill.[55]

In the fullness of time, God chose a young maiden in Nazareth to be both bride and mother. The Virgin Mary was deemed worthy of this highest calling by her faithfulness and chastity. Whereas Adam named his wife Eve, the mother of the living, God has made Mary, the Theotokos, the Mother of all Christians. Whereas all the living are kin to Adam through his blood and sin, all Christians are kin to Christ, the New Adam, through His Blood and faithfulness.

For just as from the rib of Adam He made woman, so from the daughter of Adam, the Ever-Virgin Mother of God Mary, He borrowed the virginal flesh without seed, and being clothed in it, became man like unto the first-created Adam, so as to accomplish this work, namely: just as Adam, through the transgression of the commandment of God was the cause of the fact that all men became corruptible and mortal, so also Christ, the new Adam, through the fulfillment of justice, became the first-

---

[55] LOE, #38, p. 79.

fruit of our rebirth into incorruption and immortality.[56]

And Eve sang: My heart leaps with pride and triumphant joy in beholding Mary, my long hoped-for daughter: how by her meekness, love, purity, and obedience she reversed my great sins of pride, apostasy, adultery, and disobedience. By the virginity and kenosis – willing sacrifice – of her spirit, soul and body, God deemed her meet to bear our Savior: He who by His death on the tree of the cross reversed the sin Adam and I committed through the tree. My soul will forever praise her example: a handmaiden of God, a helpmate for mankind to all eternity, subservient with joy to the will of her Master.[57]

For Christ, the New Adam, and Mary, the New Eve, there was also a tree, the Tree of Life, the Cross. This Tree, which St Ephraim the Syrian poetically describes as the very tree of life from Genesis, sprouted forth on Calvary.

In place of the tree of knowledge, there was the Cross; in place of the stepping of the feet by which our first ancestors walked to a forbidden tree, and in place of their stretching out of their hands in

---

[56] TFCM, p. 96.
[57] LOE, #9, p. 106.

order to take of the fruit of the tree, there
were nailed to the Cross the innocent feet
and hands of Christ; in place of the
tasting of the fruit, there was the tasting
of gall and vinegar, and in place of the
death of Adam, the death of Christ.[58]

Since Adam had fallen under the curse,
and through him all people also who
proceed from him, therefore the sentence
of God concerning this could in no way
be annihilated; and therefore Christ was
for us a curse, through being hung upon
the tree of the Cross, so as to offer
Himself as a sacrifice to His Father, as has
been said, and to annihilate the sentence
of God by the superabundant worth of
the sacrifice.[59]

And it is here that we observe a great and terrible
mystery, Christ became sin for us (2 Cor. 5:21). He, the
fashioner of the universe, as He hung on the Tree, became
the saving serpent (the One Who undoes the evil serpent
of old) foreshadowed by the staff of Moses in the desert[60]
– "And as Moses lifted up the serpent in the wilderness, so
must the Son of man be lifted up, that whoever believes in
Him may have eternal life" (Jn. 3:14-15).

Divine things are very often prefigured by
means of shadowy types. Typology points
out what is to be expected, indicating

---

[58] TFCM, p. 46.
[59] TFCM, p. 47.
[60] Num. 21:4–9.

through imitation what is to happen before it happens. Adam was a type of Him who was to come;[61] "the Rock was Christ"[62] typologically, and the water from the rock was a type of living power of the Word, for He says, "If anyone thirst, let him come to Me and drink."[63] The manna was a type of the living bread which came down from heaven,[64] and the serpent suspended on the pole[65] was a type of the saving passion accomplished on the cross, since the life of every one who looked at the serpent was preserved.[66]

The Cross was therefore the image of Moses' staff, our Lord the serpent. Though without sin, He became sin. Whereas, the tree of transgression was the door to our exit from Paradise; Christ has transformed the tree of humiliation into the very ladder to Paradise.[67]

---

[61] Rom. 5:14.

[62] 1 Cor. 10:4.

[63] Jn. 7:37.

[64] Jn. 6:41.

[65] Num. 21:8ff.

[66] St. Basil the Great, *On the Holy Spirit* (Crestwood, New York: St. Vladimir's Seminary Press, 1980), p. 53.

[67] The teaching is clear. For if the father of sin is called a serpent by Holy Scripture and what is born of the serpent is certainly a serpent, it follows that sin is synonymous with the one who begot it. But the apostolic word testifies that the Lord was made into sin for our sake by being invested with our sinful nature. This figure is rightly applied to the Lord. For if sin is a serpent and the Lord became sin, the logical conclusion should be evident to all: By becoming sin he became also a serpent, which

> For just as those who are like the old
> Adam, who transgressed the
> commandment of God, remain outside
> the Kingdom of Heaven, despite the fact
> that they are not by any means guilty of
> the fact that they are like their forefather
> Adam, so also Christians, like the New
> Adam, their father Christ, enter into the
> Kingdom of Heaven despite the fact that
> their likeness to Christ is not their own
> doing, since this is accomplished by
> means of the faith which they receive in
> Christ.[68]

And what is this likeness to Christ that we are to put on?

> The likeness of Christ consists in truth,
> meekness, righteousness, and together
> with them humility and love of
> mankind.[69]

Though the image of Adam was tarnished, our
reflection of the perfect image, which is Christ, is washed
clean through His humility and sacrifice. We, like the
Prodigal son who **came to himself,** must turn from our

---

is nothing other than sin. For our sake he became a serpent to
devour and consume the Egyptian serpents produced by the
sorcerers. This done, the serpent was changed back into a rod by
which sinners are brought to their senses, and those slackening
on the upward and toilsome course of virtue are given rest ....
- Gregory of Nyssa, *The Life of Moses*, trans. Abraham J. Malherbe
and Everett Ferguson (New York: Paulist Press, 1978), p. 124.
[68] TFCM, p. 55.
[69] TFCM, p. 55.

running astray and return to the Father. Understanding the *image* as residing in the intellect and reflecting on the parable of the Prodigal, Georgios Mantzaridis paraphrases St Gregory Palamas:

> Man's chief wealth is his inborn intellect. While he keeps to the path of salvation, he keeps his intellect concentrated in itself and on the first and highest Intellect, God. If, however, he is led astray into misuse, then his intellect is dispersed and adheres to earthly things, and to the pleasures of the flesh. Man is required to fight against this pathological deviation through his return to himself and elevation towards God.[70]

> If there exists something that man can and must seek and find within himself, it is not the self which deviated but the new man in Christ, born through baptismal grace and the other church sacraments.[71]

Thus, we do not come to our base nature – *the old man* – which is corrupted by sin. Rather, we come to that which is good, beautiful, and true. We come to that which Adam was before the Fall; we come to the New Man, Christ, Who is within us.

---

[70] Georgios I. Mantzarides, *The Deification of Man: St Gregory Palamas and the Orthodox Tradition*, trans. Liadain Sherrard (Crestwood, New York: St. Vladimir's Seminary Press, 1997), p. 82.
[71] TDOM, p. 83

A carnal man's mind is not trained in
contemplation, but remains buried in the
mud of the fleshly lusts, powerless to look
up and see the spiritual light of truth. So
the "world" – life enslaved by carnal
passions – can no more receive the grace
of the Spirit than a weak eye can look at
the light of a sunbeam.[72]

We are called to "put on Christ." We are to
become like God, thereby regaining the "likeness" that we
lost by transgression. The first step in this process is that
we "come to ourselves." This coming to oneself is the first
step toward repentance and reconciliation that leads to
communion with God and neighbor. This is true when
"man, 'having entered wholly within himself, becomes
aware of himself and awaits within himself the coming of
God and the divine transformation."[73]

Certainly, we all have some discernment.
Let us not kid ourselves that we are in
good standing with God even though we
neglect our neighbor and we are living the
life of the "old man." Let us put on the
New Man and "resolve to struggle
fervently, cut off our passions, liberate
our soul, and fly into Heaven."[74]

The following prayer, the work of St Ephraim the
Syrian addressed to the Second Eve, the Theotokos

---

[72] St Basil, p. 84.
[73] TDOM, p. 85.
[74] Elder Paisius, pp. 150-151.

exemplifies our need to cleanse our minds — setting aright those passions that stain us:

> O most holy Mother of God, O only Lady who art utterly pure in both soul and body, look upon me, abominable and unclean, who have blackened soul and body with the stains of my passionate and gluttonous life. Cleanse my passionate mind; set aright my blind and wandering thoughts and make them incorrupt; bring my senses to order and guide them; free me from my evil and repulsive addiction to unclean prejudices and passions which torment me; grant my clouded and wretched mind the sobriety and discernment to correct my intentions and failings that, freed from the darkness of sin, I might be worthy to boldly glorify and praise thee, O only true Mother of the true Light, Christ our God; for all creation, visible and invisible, blesses and glorifies thee, both with Him and in Him.[75]

By God's grace, the correction of our "intentions and failings" can transform even the Passions. We may take pride in God's creation, be angry at the fallen angels, lust after virtue, envy the virtues of the heavenly hosts, be gluttonous of the good things of God, horde the bounty of charity, and be slothful toward transgression (etc).

---

[75] Ephraim the Syrian, *A Spiritual Psalter or Reflections on God*, trans. Isaac Lambertson (Liberty, Tennessee: St. John of Kronstadt Press, 1997), p. 63.

The Struggle: Lists, Naughty and Nice

*One should try to discover what stage one is at,
where our desires tend, and what our dislike is
aimed at. A catalogue of virtues and vices will
render great service. 'Anger, for example: does
one suppress it with some and give vent to it with
others? ... or sadness: does one overcome it for
certain things, but not for others, or in everything?
It is the same for fear and the other vices that are
opposed to the virtues', and so on.[76]*

*In writing about the stages of the mystical ascent
to God, St Maximos the Confessor mentions
both "practical philosophy which is both negative
(purification from passions) and positive
(acquisition of virtues)."[77]*

Most of us are familiar with the practice of
dividing a piece of paper into two columns: Good and
Bad, Pro and Con.[78] The goal of such an exercise is, of

---

[76] Irénée Hausherr, *Spiritual Direction in the Early Christian East*,
trans. Anthony P. Gythiel (Kalamazoo, Michigan: Cistercian
Publications, 1990; original French edition, 1955), p. 224.
[77] Hierotheos Vlachos, *A Night in the Desert of the Holy Mountain*,
trans. Effie Mavromichali (Greece: Birth of the Theotokos
Monastery, 1991), p. 119.
[78] This device, entitled "Yay Uh-Oh Lists," was employed within
the weeklong curriculum of the Two Trees at Camp St. Thecla,
Nashville, Tennessee, in 2005. The cabin counselors would keep
a daily log of virtues and vices displayed by the campers each
day. At the next morning's breakfast, the counselors would read
off the edifying portions of the lists to help the campers to
appreciate the Two Trees theme.

course, to encourage the good and help eliminate the bad. This practice may also be used in preparing for Confession. Whereas cursory use of the Ten Commandments in preparing for Confession may bear only a small amount of bitter fruit, using a Virtue-Vice list is much more comprehensive.

Such listings of virtues and vices were common in the ancient Mediterranean world; they are also found in the Gospels, St Paul's Epistles, and the writings of early Church Fathers. Reviewing such lists – especially making one's own – can be helpful in preparing for Confession.

Virtue lists in the New Testament:

2 Corinthians 6:6-7a
Galatians 5:22-23
Ephesians 4:2-3, 32-5:2
Philippians 4:8
Colossians 3:12
1 Timothy 3:2-4, 8-10, 11-12; 4:12; 6:11, 18
2 Timothy 2:22-25; 3:10
Titus 1:8; 2:2-10
Hebrews 7:26
1 Peter 3:8
2 Peter 1:5-7
1 Corinthians 13:4-7

Vice lists in the New Testament:

Matthew 15:19
Mark 7:21-22
Romans 1:29-31; 13:13
1 Corinthians 5:10-11; 6:9-10
2 Corinthians 12:20-21

Galatians 5:19-21
Ephesians 4:31; 5:3-5
Colossians 3:5-8
1 Timothy 1:9-10; 6:4-5
2 Timothy 3:2-4
Titus 1:7; 3:3
1 Peter 2:1; 4:3, 15
Revelation 9:21; 21:8; 22:15[79]

These lists serve as an aid to proper development of conduct and moral character. In some instances (particularly the morality plays of the Middle Ages), vices and virtues were personified. Here, the Vices are depicted as the fruit of the Tree of the Knowledge of Good and Evil; the Virtues as the fruit of the Tree of Life.

> On the tree of knowledge was a mixture of good and bad fruit. And the bad fruit was more attractive, as always, not only in taste, but in appearance, with bright colors and beautiful shapes. Deluded, curious, the woman reached out and ate first the fruit of evil and then the fruit of good. Because of this, she first gave birth to the bad Cain and then the good Abel. And from then on they continued to bear both bad and good, through all the ages and generations of men. Estrangements, conflicts, quarrels, wars filled the whole history of mankind. The history of the

---

[79] David Noel Freedman (ed.), *Anchor Bible Dictionary* (New York: Doubleday, 1992), pp. 857-859.

world is a macrocosm of the Tree of Knowledge.[80]

Ancient philosophers used such lists as teaching tools. Both passions and vices proper were mentioned in Stoic vice lists, which were often used to describe and castigate the sinful and irrational life led by the masses or by particular individuals. Whereas vice lists thus depict the deficient life that fails to achieve its human potential, virtue lists paint and praise the ideal, whether that of the ideal manner of life or of some ideal figure, such as that of the wise man or the good sovereign.[81]

St Paul's use of catalogues of virtues and vices must stem from pre-Pauline catechetical instruction. The reason for this is evident in the moral of such lists: "People who do such things will not inherit the kingdom of God."[82] However, since St Paul rarely uses the "kingdom of God" in his teaching, it may be that he inherited such teaching from Hellenistic philosophical writings and Palestinian Jewish texts.[83]

These catalogues, or lists, of virtues-vices grew up within Hellenic Jewish circles to include the evils of the Gentile way of life as viewed from a Jewish perspective. Included in such lists would be, of course, "idolatry," and "impurity," and such Greek terms as *komoi* (unbridled festivities) which described pagan religious rites – even orgies. These lists were then used to attract Gentiles to

---

[80] LOE, #40, p. 83.

[81] Freedman, p. 857.

[82] Galatians 5:21.

[83] Occurring only in 1 Thessalonians 2:12; 1 Corinthians 4:20; 6:9-10; 15:24, 50; Romans 14:17. - Brown, Raymond E., et. al. (eds.), *The New Jerome Bible Commentary* (Englewood Cliffs, New Jersey: Prentice Hall, 1990), p. 1413.

Judaism. They came in handy for the early Church missionaries, who used them to influence the behavior of converts. According to Tarazi, it is evident that St Paul edited these lists to fit particular situations which he was addressing in the churches.[84]

Within a Christian context, Christ is the One who fulfills the ideal. Christians are called to imitate Christ. For example, St Paul writes to the Galatians: "The fruit of the Spirit, on the other hand, is love, joy, peace, forbearance/patience, kindness, goodness, faithfulness, gentleness, self-control, against such there is no law."[85] It should be noted that "love" is the only part of the list which is not included in the Hellenistic catalogues. Here we see the Christian novelties of "love" and the "Spirit," which were both introduced in the first century A.D.[86] This notion, that Christ is to be imitated by Christians, is clearly reflected in the second set of "virtues" (forbearance/patience, kindness, goodness). All three are basically divine attributes applicable to the Christian person only secondarily, insofar as he models himself after Christ and God.[87] Because Adam believed the devil who

---

[84] Paul Tarazi and Paul Nadim, *Galatians, A Commentary* (Crestwood, New York: St. Vladimir's Seminary Press, 1994), p. 295.

[85] Tarazi, p. 297.

[86] Tarazi, p. 297.

[87] "The first, *makroqumia* (forbearance/patience), is specifically related to God's judgment (Rom 2:3-5; 9:22-23), a divine activity par excellence. 'Kindness' is almost always directly linked to 'forbearance' (Rom 2:4; 2 Cor 6:6; Gal 5:22; see also 1 Cor 13:4). All three terms ... when applied to God, refer to what is essentially one notion regarding His attitude toward and dealings with mankind. Since for Paul the first two terms are linked to the notion of divine judgment, he means here not only that one must patiently/forbearingly/persistently act in accordance with

had told him his lies, and tasted of the tree of knowledge, therefore, as one who had believed a liar, he fell away from the truth. After this, human nature labored a great deal seeking the truth but could not find it. This is clearly confirmed by all the wise men of Greece, who could by no means harmonize, unify, and direct on the right path the varieties of human wisdom, despite the fact that many used means for this end and wrote a multitude of lengthy works in which they examined virtue and vice from all points of view.[88]

---

goodness/kindness (6:9-10; see 1 Thess 5:15), but also that in doing so one must not take thought for any immediate rewards. What one sows one will surely reap, but reaping comes later, on the last Day (6:7-8)." Tarazi, pp. 297-299.

[88] TFCM, p. 67.

Passions and Virtues

He does not destroy all our passions at once, but leaves them in us, letting them fight against us till our very death, for just the same purpose, namely, to prove our love for Him and our obedience to His will, and to train us in spiritual warfare.[89]

Postlapsarian humanity – Man after the Fall – is now subject to the Passions. The Passions are demons with which we all struggle. St John Climacus affirms that God is not the creator of the passions and that they are "unnatural," alien to Man's true self.[90] While some Fathers include the sin of Vainglory, most lists of the Passions include what is commonly referred to as the Seven Deadly (Cardinal) Sins: Pride, Anger, Lust, Envy, Gluttony, Avarice, and Sloth.

By ridding ourselves of the Passions, by way of the Holy Spirit we may acquire their antidotes, the Virtues.[91] The opposite of the seven grievous sins, the Seven Capital Virtues are: Humility, Patience, Chastity, Contentedness, Temperance, Liberality, and Diligence. There are many fruits of the Holy Spirit enumerated in Scripture. These are "powers and possessions of the mind and the heart which all people should have if they are truly human, fulfilling themselves as created in the image and likeness of God."[92]

---

[89] Lorenzo Scupoli, *Unseen Warfare: The Spiritual Combat and Path to Paradise*, ed. Nicodemus of the Holy Mountain, rev. Theophan the Recluse (Crestwood, New York: St. Vladimir's Seminary Press, 1997), p. 112.

[90] Cf. LDA, Step 26, pp. 161-197.

[91] See Appendix IV for a note on the Holy Spirit and Grace.

[92] Hopko, p. 56.

As with the fulfillment of Psalm 1 and the Beatitudes (which will be discussed later), the Virtues are actually attributes of God. They exist in human beings by virtue of being created in God's image, after God's likeness. Yet, due to our fallen nature, we must (re)acquire the Virtues by way of Christ's salvation.[93] Here, again, the process by which Orthodox Christians rid themselves of the Passions and progress toward the Virtues requires repentance. For, how is it possible to be filled with light when one is possessed by darkness? The fruits of the Spirit require obedience to God. Yet, if we are continually found in disobedience, how shall we acquire them? St Paul writes:

> Finally, brethren, whatever is true, whatever is honorable, whatever is just, whatever is pure, whatever is lovely, whatever is gracious, if there is any excellence, if there is anything worthy of praise, think about these things (Phil. 4:8).

---

[93] "It has been said, and it is true, that the Christian virtues are not all particularly 'Christian' in the sense that only Christians know about them and are committed to attain them. Most, if not all, of the Christian virtues have been honored, respected and recommended by all great teachers of the spiritual life. This in no way detracts from their Christian value and truth, for Christ and His apostles and saints have not taught and practiced something other than that which all men should teach and practice. As the fulfillment of all positive human aspirations and desires, it is quite understandable that Jesus Christ, the perfect 'man from heaven' and 'final Adam' (1 Corinthians 15:45-47; Romans 5:14), should fulfill and realize in Himself that which all men of wisdom and good-will have sought for and desired in their minds and hearts, enlightened by God" (Hopko, p. 56).

Yet, how is it possible to follow this exhortation when our hearts and minds are often darkened by the very antithesis of St Paul's words? The darkness, the Passion, must be removed in order for the light, the Virtues, to spring forth. The gifts of God, the fruits of the Spirit, are freely given, but we must prepare to receive them. For this to occur, we must discern the difference between Virtue and Vice.

The Passions

PRIDE is operative when we place our own needs above all others – including God. Every sin is a form of pride. St John Climacus states:

> Pride is denial of God, an invention of the devil, the despising of men, the mother of condemnation, the offspring of praise, a sign of sterility, flight from Divine assistance, the precursor of madness, the cause of falls, a foothold for satanic possession, a source of anger, a door of hypocrisy, the support of demons, the guardian of sins, the patron of pitilessness, the rejection of compassion, a bitter inquisitor, an inhuman judge, an opponent of God, a root of blasphemy. [94]

---

[94] LDA, p. 138.

Aside from vainglory, pride is the mother of all passions.[95] There is no sin with which pride is not involved. Pride is the lie which the Serpent spoke from the Tree: "You will be like God …."[96] Believing this, humanity has continually to struggle with pride. It should be noted, however, that God is humble. This is the ultimate deception. For in our constant consumption of pride we actually become less like God.

Despair and despondency are the *flipside* of pride. That is, when we believe things should be a certain way (pride) and over and over again our fantasies are dashed, we often fall into despair and despondency.

> Just as marriage and a funeral are the very opposite of each other, so too are pride and despair. But as a result of confusion caused by the demons, it is possible to see the two together.[97]

ANGER is the result of people not doing or saying what we wish or when things are not going the way we prefer. Rather than adapt to circumstances by way of the practice of patience, we often succumb to the sin of anger. Paramount in the equation of anger is the "remembrance of wrongs." St John Climacus writes:

> The holy virtues are like Jacob's ladder, and the unholy vices are like the chains that fell from the chief Apostle Peter.

---

[95] St. John Climacus claims that "vainglory" is the mother of the passions. Yet, for the purposes of this project, this passion is joined with the sin of pride.
[96] Gen. 3:5b.
[97] LDA, p. 185.

For the virtues, leading from one to another, bear him who chooses them up to Heaven, but the vices by their very nature beget and stifle one another. And as we have just heard senseless anger calling remembrance of wrongs its own offspring, it is appropriate that we should now say something about this.[98]

An essential element fueling our "remembrance of wrongs" is in not forgiving, forgetting, or practicing long-suffering with our fellow strugglers. Instead, we allow the Enemy to continuously beat us up with remembering the many wrongs (real and imagined) committed against us.

Remembrance of wrongs is the consummation of anger, the keeper of sins, hatred of righteousness, ruin of virtues, poison of the soul, worm of the mind, shame of prayer, cessation of supplication, estrangement of love, a nail stuck in the soul, pleasureless feeling cherished in the sweetness of bitterness, continuous sin, unsleeping transgression, hourly malice.[99]

Then Peter came to Him and said, "Lord, how often shall my brother sin against me, and I forgive him? Up to seven times?" Jesus said to him, "I do not say

---

[98] LDA, p. 87.
[99] LDA, p. 87.

to you, up to seven times, but up to seventy times seven." (Mt. 18:21-22)

While not at the top of the "most grievous list," the pervasiveness of this sin warrants special mention. We live in an age where, though we have less and less direct contact with others, we seem so easily tempted by thoughts, feelings, fantasies, and injuries believed caused by our neighbor.

Whenever we become obsessed by some past event in which we perceive that we have been wronged, we give the devil ample opportunity to lead us toward greater temptation. We forget that our warfare is not with each other! We are to engage in spiritual warfare against the Enemy of our salvation and his willing hosts, the demons. When we remember wrongs, we fall prey to the Father of Lies and engage in combat with our fellow brothers and sisters. St John of Kronstadt writes:

> The Devil cunningly induces us – instead of irritating us against himself – to notice our neighbors' sins, to make us spiteful and angry with others, and to awaken our contempt towards them, thus keeping us in enmity with our neighbors, and with the Lord God Himself. Therefore, we must despise the sins, the faults themselves, and not our brother who commits them at the Devil's instigation, through infirmity and habit; we must pity him, and gently and lovingly instruct him, as one who forgets himself, or who is sick, as a prisoner and the slave of his sin. But our animosity, our anger towards the

sinner only increases his sickness, oblivion, and spiritual bondage, instead of lessening them; besides this, it make us ourselves like madmen, or sick men, the prisoners of our own passions, and of the Devil, who is the author of them.[100]

The victory over this plague, remembrance of wrongs, is true repentance and a sincere struggle to love.

The forgetting of wrongs is a sign of true repentance. But he who dwells on them and thinks that he is repenting is like a man who thinks he is running while he is really sleeping.[101]

How true! We can expend a great amount of energy in being, and remaining, mad at someone. Nursing enmities gives birth to sleeplessness, mental and emotional preoccupation, thoughts of evil, and worse. True love, God-pleasing love, bears the sweet fruits of repentance, forgiveness, compassion, and charity.

True love willingly bears privations, troubles, and labours; endures offenses, humiliations, defeats, sins, and injustices, if they do not harm others; bears patiently and meekly the baseness and malice of

---

[100] Saint John of Kronstadt, *MY LIFE in CHRIST or Moments of Spiritual Serenity and Contemplation, of Reverent Feeling, of Earnest Self-Amendment, and of Peace in God: Extracts from the Diary of St. John of Kronstadt*, trans. E. E. Goulaeff (Jordanville, New York: Holy Trinity Monastery, 1994), p. 166.
[101] LDA, p. 89.

> others, leaving judgment to the all-seeing
> God, the righteous Judge, and praying
> that He may teach those who are
> darkened by senseless passions.[102]

As the saying goes, "The desire to believe the best of people is a prerequisite for intercourse with strangers; suspicion is reserved for friends." It often happens that those closest to us cause us the most harm; those we help the most are the ones hurting us more, etc. It's only "natural," you step on the toes of those with whom you are dancing. Thus, our best face is reserved for strangers. We let down our guard and show our worst side to our loved ones. We slip into rudeness with our intimates, thinking, "Oh, it's okay ... they know me." Talk about Opposite Day!

Essentially, we are practicing a form of deception. We want strangers to think that we are better than we actually are. In essence, we do not trust ourselves. We wish to avoid rejection, we desire respect, and, thus, we try to appear different from what we really are. When we are assured of another's approval, then we tend to drop our guard.

This would all serve its desired purpose, were it not for our fallen nature. The thing about deception is that it is never true! For us to be in a right relationship with God and neighbor, it is essential for us to be open, honest and trusting.

> It may happen that someone, having
> sincerely repented, will obtain mercy from
> God and receive the forgiveness of all his

---

[102] Kronstadt, p. 236.

debt of sin; but if after this he will be uncompassionate and unmerciful to others and will not forgive them in whatever they have sinned against him, he himself will dissolve the merciful condescension of God to him as well as the forgiveness which was manifested to him by God, as the Holy Gospel says: "Shouldst not thou also have had mercy on thy fellow-servant, even as I had mercy on thee? And his lord was wroth, and delivered him to the tormentors" (Mt. 18:33-34).[103]

It is in the family of God, the Church, that we find forgiveness from God. Yet the unfaithful servant, after gaining the Grace of God's forgiveness, lost it all when he failed to forgive in return. We too can lose everything that we have been given (and forgiven) by God in that terrible moment when we refuse to forgive our debtors. We receive forgiveness in the Sacrament of Confession. We receive Grace in the Sacrament of Holy Communion. And in one moment, that moment when we turn our back, walk out on God, and demand of our debtors that which we have been forgiven – we lose it all.

We must be vigilant in our repentance, our forgetting of wrongs and hurt feelings. Let us put aside our weapons used for mutual destruction and embrace the Love that is Christ in order to do God-pleasing warfare with the Enemy of our salvation.

---

[103] TFCM, p. 85.

If you suffer some injustice or injury,
some loss or affliction, do not forget to
give thanks for it to God, since, being
sent in accordance with God's will, which
is always good, it is visiting you for your
own benefit.[104]

"Love thy neighbor as thyself." It was
given to me to understand this
commandment in the form of a gigantic
tree, of cosmic dimensions, whose root is
Adam. Myself, I am only a little leaf on a
branch of this tree. But this tree is not
foreign to me; it is the basis of my being.
I belong to it. To pray for the whole
world is to pray for this tree in its totality,
with its milliards of leaves.[105]

LUST means to look at another with sexual
longing. This may also be coupled with sensual imaginings
from the past or totally contrived fantasies with no
connection to real events. In the modern world of
electronic visual images (television, internet, billboards,
etc), it is a daily struggle to avert the eyes from portrayal of
sexual images. This can lead to even greater falls.

The snake of sensuality is many-faced. In
those who are inexperienced in sin, he
sows the thought of making one trial and
then stopping. But this crafty creature

---

[104] UW, p. 203.
[105] Archimandrite Sophrony (Sakharov), *Words of Life*, trans.
Sister Magdalen (Essex: Stavropegic Monastery of St. John the
Baptist, 1996), p. 16.

incites those who have tried this to fresh trial through the remembrance of their sin. Many inexperienced people feel no conflict in themselves simply because they do not know what is bad; and the experienced, because they know this abomination, suffer disquiet and struggle. But often the opposite of this also happens.[106]

While the passion of lust has been prevalent since the Fall, it has increased in intensity in these latter days. Consider this writing from St John of the Ladder:

> The good Lord shows His great care for us in the shamelessness that the feminine sex is checked by shyness as with a sort of bit. For if the woman were to run after the man, no flesh would be saved.[107]

ENVY is not only wanting something that someone else has, it is hating them for having it. Envy seems to fuel consumerism in our society. How can we escape this sin living in the modern world of capitalism and commercialism? Can we imagine watching television or surfing the internet while obeying the Tenth Commandment?

> You shall not covet your neighbor's house; you shall not covet your neighbor's wife, or his manservant, or his

---

[106] Sophrony, p. 115.
[107] Sophrony, p. 115.

maidservant, or his ox, or his ass, or anything that is your neighbor's (Ex. 20:17).

GLUTTONY is not just overeating. It is the inordinate desire of things sensate; that is, an obsession with things which stimulate the senses. Gluttony may, therefore, be experienced in talking too much, having itching ears, overeating, drinking and smoking in excess, watching too much television, wasting time on the internet, listening to too much radio, etc. Gluttony – especially of food and drink – leads to a multitude of other sins.

> And gluttony replies: "Why are you, who are my underlings, overwhelming me with reproaches? Why are you trying to escape from me? I am bound to you by nature. The door for me is the nature of foods. The cause of my insatiability is habit. The foundation of my passion is repeated habit, insensibility of soul and forgetfulness of death. How do you seek to learn the names of my offspring? If I count them, they will be more in number than the sand. But learn at least the names of my first-born and beloved children. My first born son is a minister of fornication, the second after him is hardness of heart, and the third is sleepiness."[108]

---

[108] LDA, pp. 102-103.

AVARICE is an old-fashioned word for "greed," that is, the accumulation and overabundance of material wealth (e.g., theft, dishonesty, misrepresentation, or sharing of stolen goods; cheating in business, taxes, school or games). Avarice makes worldly success the goal of our life or the standard for judging others.[109] According to the writings of the Fathers, greed leads to despondency. St John Climacus states: "Despondency is born sometimes of luxury, and sometimes of vainglory."[110] We hardly notice avarice as evil, living in America in this day and age. It is, rather like pride, often touted as a virtue.

SLOTH is not just laziness; rather, it can also be a shirking of God-pleasing duties. For example, a man may travel around the world with business dealings and provide financial wealth to his family – all the while being a slothful husband and father. One can also fall prey to slothfulness in prayer, fasting, and almsgiving.[111]

> Just as over-drinking is a matter of habit, so too from habit comes over-sleeping. Therefore we must struggle with the question of sleep, especially in the early days of obedience, because a long-standing habit is difficult to cure.[112]
>
> There is a demon who comes to us when we are lying in bed and shoots at us evil and unclean thoughts, so that when we do

---

[109] SAPB, p. 118.

[110] LDA, p. 168.

[111] SAPB defines SLOTH as "the refusal to respond to our opportunities for growth, service or sacrifice" (p. 120).

[112] LDA, pp. 126-127.

Fr Joseph David Huneycutt

not stand for prayer because of our laziness and thus are not armed against them, we may fall asleep with these foul thoughts and then have foul dreams too.[113]

All is not lost for those who have continually fallen prey to the Enemy by way of the Passions. St John Climacus writes:

> Let those who have been humbled by their passions take courage. For even if they fall into every pit and are trapped in all the snares and suffer all maladies, yet after their restoration to health they become physicians, beacons, lamps, and pilots for all, teaching us the habits of every disease and from their own personal experience able to rescue those who are about to fall.[114]

He does not, however, hide his perplexity, saying:

> One thing about us astonishes me very much: Why do we so quickly and easily incline to the passions, when we have Almighty God, angels and saints, to help us towards the virtues, and only the wicked demon against us? I do not wish to speak about this in more detail; in fact, I cannot.[115]

---

[113] LDA, p. 177.
[114] LDA, p. 163.
[115] LDA, p. 182.

The Virtues[116]

HUMILITY is the remedy of the Passions.[117] While the Passions are the result of disobedience, the Virtues are the fruit of obedience.[118] St John Climacus states that holy obedience is the "mother of all virtues."[119] And, it seems almost impossible to speak of obedience without humility.

> Our treatise now appropriately touches upon warriors and athletes of Christ. As the flower precedes the fruit, so exile, either of the body or of the will, always precedes obedience. For with the help of these two virtues, the holy soul steadily ascends to Heaven as upon golden wings. And perhaps it was about this that he

---

[116] St. John Climacus notes: "There are inclinations which are considered virtues, yet are not, but are really gifts and advantages of nature. Many people are naturally meek, gentle, sober, courageous, modest, chaste, or silent. It is no virtue to be naturally a small eater; but it is a virtue to abstain voluntarily and by choice" (LDA, p. 135).

[117] "All the contrary virtues are born of parents contrary to these. But without enlarging the subject (for I should not have time if I were to inquire into them all one by one), I will merely say that for all the passions mentioned above, the remedy is humility. Those who have obtained that virtue have overcome all" (LDA, p. 169).

[118] "The fathers have laid down that psalmody is a weapon, and prayer is a wall, and honest tears are a bath; but blessed obedience in their judgment is confession of faith, without which no one subject to passions will see the Lord" (LDA, p. 23).

[119] LDA, xliii.

who received the Holy Spirit sang: "Who
will give me wings like a dove? And I will
fly by activity, and be at rest by divine
vision and humility."[120]

Forgetfulness of our falls is the result of
conceit, for the remembrance of them
leads to humility.[121]

The natural property of the lemon tree is
such that it lifts its branches upwards
when it has no fruit, but the more the
branches bend down the more fruit they
bear. Those who have the mind to
understand will grasp the meaning of
this.[122]

PATIENCE, in my experience, both as fellow
struggler and pastor, is the Virtue most lacking in
contemporary life. While other Passions may afflict us just
as equally; anger seems to spring up so suddenly that our
lack of patience is continuously and immediately on
display. How does one acquire the Virtue of Patience?
The Elder Joseph the Hesychast writes:

However, if you get angry with your
fellow brothers, or get in a rage and ruin
the works of your hands, know that you
are suffering from vainglory and are
abusing the nerve of your soul. You are

---

[120] LDA, p. 20.
[121] LDA, p. 141.
[122] LDA, p. 157.

delivered from this passion through love towards all humanity and true humility.

Therefore, when anger comes, close your mouth tightly and do not speak to him who curses, dishonors, reproaches, or bothers you in any way without reason. Then this snake will writhe around in your heart, rise up to your throat, and (since you don't give it a way out) will choke and suffocate. When this is repeated several times, it will diminish and cease entirely.[123]

St John Climacus exhorts:

Bring out the staff of patience, and the dogs will soon stop their insolence. Patience is an unbroken labour of the soul which is never shaken by deserved or undeserved blows. The patient man is a faultless worker, who turns his faults into victories. Patience is the limitation of suffering that is accepted day by day. Patience lays aside all excuses and all attention to herself. The worker needs patience more than his food, because the one brings him a crown, while the other may bring ruin. The patient man has died long before he is placed in the tomb ... Hope engenders patience and so does

---

[123] Elder Joseph the Hesychast, *Monastic Wisdom* (Florence, Arizona: St Anthony's Greek Orthodox Monastery, 1998), pp. 61-62.

mourning, but he who has neither is a slave to despondency.[124]

CHASTITY refers not only to abstinence from sexual sin, but to faithfulness in all things. Thus, "Chastity is the name which is common to all the virtues."[125] In Orthodoxy, this Virtue is best pursued by keeping vigil both in church and in personal spiritual warfare.

> Vigil is a quenching of lust, deliverance from dream phantasies, a tearful eye, a softened heart, the guarding of thoughts, the smelting furnace of food, the subduing of passions, the taming of spirits, the chastisement of the tongue, the banishment of phantasies.[126]

It is also a byproduct of humility.

> Offer to the Lord the weakness of your nature, fully acknowledge your own powerlessness, and imperceptibly you will receive the gift of chastity.[127]

CONTENTEDNESS is the culmination of desire. Created in God's image and trusting in God's care, we are called to be content with our station in life. Each moment is provided for our spiritual benefit and salvation. Yet, in our disobedience, we tend to spend more time dwelling on the past or dreading the future than we do in

---

[124] LDA, p. 209.
[125] LDA, p. 104.
[126] LDA, p. 158.
[127] LDA, p. 106.

appreciating and partaking of the present moment. St Paul writes:

> Keep your life free from love of money, and be content with what you have, for he has said, "I will never fail you nor forsake you" (Heb. 13:5).

Supremely, our Lord exhorts us thus:

> Therefore I tell you, do not be anxious about your life, what you shall eat or what you shall drink, nor about your body, what you shall put on. Is not life more than food, and the body more than clothing? Look at the birds of the air: they neither sow nor reap nor gather into barns, and yet your heavenly Father feeds them. Are you not of more value than they? And which of you by being anxious can add one cubit to his span of life? And why are you anxious about clothing? Consider the lilies of the field, how they grow; they neither toil nor spin; yet I tell you, even Solomon in all his glory was not arrayed like one of these. But if God so clothes the grass of the field, which today is alive and tomorrow is thrown into the oven, will he not much more clothe you, O men of little faith? Therefore do not be anxious, saying, "What shall we eat?" or "What shall we drink?" or "What shall we wear?" For the Gentiles seek all these things; and your heavenly Father knows

that you need them all. But seek first his kingdom and his righteousness, and all these things shall be yours as well (Mt. 6:25-33).

Thus like Martha,[128] we too are often consumed so much with the cares of the world that we fail to seek the Kingdom of Christ. Our first step toward this Virtue is in putting away all worldly cares and trusting in the providence of God.

TEMPERANCE: In all things, we should practice moderation. In the Church, we are encouraged and aided in attaining this Virtue by way of fasting.[129] We should fast not only from foods, for: "One who had never eaten was cast from Heaven."[130] But we should fast from all those things which sever our communion with God.

> Fasting is the coercion of nature and the cutting out of everything that delights the palate, the excision of lust, the uprooting of bad thoughts, deliverance from incontinence in dreams, purity in prayer, the light of the soul, the guarding of the mind, deliverance from blindness, the

---

[128] See Luke 10:38-42.

[129] Nearly 50% of the Orthodox calendar days are Fast Days (almost all Wednesdays and Fridays, and four great Fasts: Great Lent, the Apostles' Fast, the Dormition, and the Nativity). This does not necessarily indicate total abstinence from food; rather, it entails the elimination of certain categories (meat, dairy, fish, wine, and oil) and/or a curtailing of the number of daily meals taken.

[130] LDA, p. 106.

door of compunction, humble sighing,
glad contrition, a cessation of chatter, a
cause of stillness, a guard of obedience,
lightening of sleep, health of body, agent
of dispassion, remission of sins, the gate
of Paradise and its delight.[131]

Temperance is, of course, not only fasting.
However, the Church teaches that it is by fasting that we
are perfected in this Virtue.

While struggling against all the passions,
let us who are in communities struggle
every hour, especially against these two:
greed of stomach and irritability. For in a
community there is plenty of food for
these passions.[132]

LIBERALITY entails freely giving of that which
we have received. What is required first, however, is our
sacrificial gift of our selves to the Lord. A priest is one
who is set apart to sacrifice. As part of the Priesthood of
all believers, we must all offer *all* to the Lord.

We want you to know, brethren, about
the grace of God which has been shown
in the churches of Macedonia, for in a
severe test of affliction, their abundance
of joy and their extreme poverty have
overflowed in a wealth of liberality on
their part. For they gave according to

---

[131] LDA, p. 102.
[132] LDA, p. 52.

their means, as I can testify, and beyond
their means, of their own free will,
begging us earnestly for the favor of
taking part in the relief of the saints – and
this, not as we expected, but first they
gave themselves to the Lord and to us by
the will of God (2 Cor. 8:1-5).

St Paul continues:

The point is this: he who sows sparingly
will also reap sparingly, and he who sows
bountifully will also reap bountifully.
Each one must do as he has made up his
mind, not reluctantly or under
compulsion, for God loves a cheerful
giver. And God is able to provide you
with every blessing in abundance, so that
you may always have enough of
everything and may provide in abundance
for every good work (2 Cor. 9:6-8).

DILIGENCE is not only earnest labour,
vigilance, and godly zeal, but "watchfulness." Elder
Joseph the Hesychast writes: "Watchfulness is unceasing
attentiveness, alertness, or vigilance whereby one keeps
watch over one's inward thoughts and fantasies, so that
they do not enter the heart."[133]

An energetic soul rouses the demons
against itself. But as our conflicts increase,
so do our crowns. He who has never

---

[133] Elder Joseph, p. 410.

been struck by the enemy will certainly not be crowned. But the warrior who does not flinch despite his incidental flaws will be glorified by the angels as a champion.[134]

When the soul betrays itself and loses the blessed and longed-for fervor, let it carefully investigate the reason for losing it. And let it arm itself with all its longing and zeal against whatever has caused this. For the former fervor can return only through the same door through which it was lost.[135]

Regarding vigilance, Hierotheos Vlachos writes:

There are certain actions which stop the movement of the passions and do not allow them to grow, and there are other actions which subdue them and make them diminish. For instance, where desire is concerned, fasting, labour and vigil do not allow passions to grow, while withdrawal … prayer and intense longing for God subdue and make it disappear.[136]

Finally, in a quote reminiscent of the Virtue-Vice Lists, St John Climacus encourages us to continually take inventory as to where we are and what progress we are making on the ladder of the kingdom.

---

[134] LDA, p. 187.
[135] LDA, p. 7.
[136] OP, p. 286.

> In every passion, and also in the virtues,
> let us critically examine ourselves: Where
> are we? At the beginning, or in the
> middle, or at the end?[137]

> Keep track of the extent of every passion
> and of every virtue, and you will know
> what progress you are making.[138]

The ontological goal, of course, is the Kingdom. In the meantime, such spiritual struggle aims at achieving dispassion.[139]

> There is ... only one way to acquire
> conscious experience of the Spirit, and
> that is to practice the virtues, to overcome

---

[137] OP, p. 172.

[138] OP, p. 196.

[139] In ecclesiastical Greek, "dispassion" means freedom from passions through being filled with the Holy Spirit of God as a fruit of divine love. It is a state of soul in which a burning love for God and men leaves no room for selfish and animal passions (OP, p. 5).
Dispassion is achieved when all three aspects of the soul (i.e., the intelligent, appetitive, and incensive aspects) are directed towards God. It is the transfiguration of the passionate aspect of the soul (i.e., the aspect of the soul that is more vulnerable to passion names the appetitive and incensive aspects), rather than its mortification. Thus dispassion in this context does not signify a stoic indifference, but rather, a transfiguration and sanctification of the powers of the soul and eventually of the body also. Elder Joseph the Hesychast, *Monastic Wisdom* (Florence, Arizona: St Anthony's Greek Orthodox Monastery, 1998), p. 397.

the passions, and so to gain *apatheia*, 'passionlessness' or 'dispassion'.[140]

---

[140] SDECE, p. xx.

Fr Joseph David Huneycutt

Of Paramours, Love and War

paramour: *a man's mistress or a woman's lover.*

mistress: *1. a woman who rules others or has control, authority, or power over   something; specifically, (a) a woman who is head of a household or institution; (b) a woman owner of an animal or slave. 2. a woman who has intimate relations with, and often is supported by, a man for a more or less extended period of time without being married to him; paramour.*

struggle: *1. to contend or fight violently with an opponent. 2. to make great efforts or attempts; to strive; to labor; as, she struggled to overcome her prejudice.*

adultery: *2. in Scripture, all manner of lewdness or unchastity; also, idolatry or apostasy.*

chastity: *4. purity; unadulterated state; as, the chastity of the gospel. [Rare.]*[141]

In spiritual warfare, what we sometimes fail to realize is that struggle is good.   However, the world teaches us that struggle is bad. So, in our relationships, when we have a struggle without the benefit of Christ and His   Church,   without   a   pure   intent   seeking   after righteousness, and without a godly conscience, we make the wrong decisions. In time, we come to believe that the struggle is bad. Thus, every time there is a struggle, we seek either (1) to numb the struggle (through alcohol,

---

[141] Definitions paraphrased from *Webster's New Universal Unabridged Dictionary* (London: Dorset & Baber, 1979).

excessive sleeping, drugs, the internet, video games, daydreaming, movies, and other methods of escapism) instead of fighting the godly fight; or, (2) to get rid of that relationship which has, in our minds, caused us the struggle (e.g., divorce, damaged parent-child relationships, and broken friendships).

Also, in such a mobile society as ours, we do not necessarily have to form close relationships with anyone. Thanks to the telephone, the television, and the internet, we have multiplied and magnified our separation all the more. Were we to surround ourselves with those whom God has given us (family, friends, neighbors, etc.) we might find that the nature of the struggle would be different. That is, we tend to see ourselves in a truer light by those with whom we are in a relationship of mutual Christian love. Essentially, we should struggle as a family – not as individuals.

And, going back to my point, the struggle is good. We must begin with that in mind. The struggle is good. If someone confesses, "I still struggle with 'X'," the first thing that I have to remind myself, as priest and confessor, and that which I have to counsel the penitent is this: **The struggle is good**. The second thing which must be remembered is: the Enemy is not very original. The devil only uses that which works. Thus, if we have fallen before, due to a particular Passion, most likely we will be greatly tempted by it again. Warfare is waged. Yet, where there is no struggle, the battle is already won. Who do you think wins when we lay down our guard? God forbid that we allow the Enemy this victory! It is when we do not struggle that we become complacent. We become desperate. We become depressed. We become despondent. We lose hope.

When we talk about losing hope, sometimes we think of the big hope, Capital "H" hope. And some of us may say, "Well, I'll never lose capital 'H'... O-P-E." And that is the Hope that at the Last Day we shall be saved. Many people hold on to that as a "given" in their life. Then, assuming that the capital "H" hope is theirs for all eternity, little by little, they lose their salvation because they lose the small h-o-p-e-s. In other words, they surrender regarding a particular area in their spiritual struggle.

It is possible to go down the list of the Passions (Pride, Anger, Lust, Envy, Gluttony, Avarice, Sloth), and, for a few, claim "I don't have a problem with that one ... or that one...." And you can justify personal solace therein because there are a couple of ways (methods) which you don't use to your own damnation! There are actually a couple of methods that you leave behind regarding your current spiritual state, struggle, and warfare. Then, at this state of delusion, we often do something that is really, really harmful. And that is, we look upon a particular Passion (Pride, Anger, Lust, Envy, Gluttony, Avarice, or Sloth) and we surrender that area over to the Enemy of our souls. We play poker. We gamble with our salvation. We take that one Passion in which we have lost hope of overcoming and we just give in to that one. And we kid ourselves that we are, at least, monogamous. We are having a relationship with only one mistress. Or, we believe that one mistress does not constitute adultery. And, therefore, it does not constitute the only way that we can be separated from the Bridegroom.

"Thou shalt have no other gods before me" (Ex. 20:3). This is the first commandment given by God to His people. Therefore, one mistress is enough to constitute adultery. Only one paramour is necessary to damn us. And it is that one in which we have lost all hope that God can heal through our unworthy cooperation. We then live in a deluded state where we imagine ourselves in the Resurrection ... holding hands with our mistress. We can only hold hands with the Bridegroom in the Resurrection (if we are to be saved). We can have no other – capital "S" – spouse. "Thou shalt have no other gods before me." And there is one reason, one way, for which our Lord will break off His relationship with us. That is if we remain in an adulterous relationship with Pride, Anger, Lust, Envy, Gluttony, Avarice, or Sloth.

In much the same way that Christ, the New Adam, is the fulfillment of all virtue, He is also the fulfillment of the ideals found in Psalm 1.

> Blessed is the man who walks not in the counsel of the wicked, nor stands in the way of sinners, nor sits in the seat of scoffers; but his delight is in the law of the LORD, and on his law he meditates day and night. He is like a tree planted by streams of water, that yields its fruit in its season, and its leaf does not wither. In all that he does, he prospers. The wicked are not so, but are like chaff which the wind drives away. Therefore the wicked will not stand in the judgment, nor sinners in the congregation of the righteous; for the LORD knows the way of the righteous, but the way of the wicked will perish.[142]

St Basil the Great elucidates the teaching of Psalm 1 thus:

---

[142] *The Psalter According to the Seventy*, trans. Holy Transfiguration Monastery (Boston, 1987), p. 25.

Blessed, therefore, is he who did not continue in the way of sinners but passed quickly by better reasoning to a pious way of life. For there are two ways opposed to each other, the one wide and broad, the other narrow and close ... Now, the smooth and downward sloping way has a deceptive guide, a wicked demon, who drags his followers through pleasure to destruction, but the rough and steep way has a good angel, who leads his followers through the toils of virtue to a blessed end.[143]

This is the essence of the Christian struggle. The smooth and downward slope and worldly pleasure is what tempted Adam and Eve in Paradise. It is the same temptation of Christ in the desert; it is our struggle.

This same theme is evident in the writings of the early Church. For example, in "The Teaching of the Twelve Apostles" ("The Didache") we read:

There are two ways, one of life and one of death; but a great difference between the two ways. The way of life, then, is this: First, thou shalt love God who made thee; second, thy neighbor as thyself; and all things whatsoever thou wouldst should not occur to thee, thou also to another do not do. And of these

---

[143] Joanna Manley (ed.), *Grace for Grace: The Psalter and the Holy Fathers* (Menlo Park, California: Monastery Books, 1992), p. 6.

sayings the teaching is this: Bless them
that curse you, and pray for your enemies,
and fast for them that persecute you.[144]

What follows is basically a compendium of
Christ's teachings – exhorting the good. Later comes the
exhortation to eschew evil:

> And the way of death is this: First of all it
> is evil and full of curse murderers,
> adulteries, lusts, fornications, thefts,
> idolatries, magic arts, witchcraft, rapines,
> false witnessings, hypocrisies, double-
> heartedness, deceit, haughtiness,
> depravity, self-will, greediness, filthy
> talking, jealousy, over-confidence,
> loftiness, boastfulness; persecutors of the
> good, hating truth, loving a lie, not
> knowing a reward for righteousness, not
> cleaving to good nor to righteous
> judgment, watching not for what is good,
> but for that which is evil ... [Etc.] Be
> delivered, children, from all these.[145]

How is one delivered from such temptations and
trials? It is impossible for those who are fallen to walk the
path of righteousness without God's grace. This grace is
freely given but, in our sins and disobedience, we are unfit
vessels for so great a gift. We must do warfare against the
mistresses, the paramours, the Passions. We must, by

---

[144] Alexander Roberts and James Donaldson (eds.), *The Ante-
Nicene Fathers* (Grand Rapids: Eerdmans, 1989), volume 7, p.
377.
[145] ANF, vol. 7, p. 379.

God's grace, strive toward the Virtues: Humility, Patience, Chastity, Contentedness, Temperance, Liberality and Diligence. How do we do this? As with any God-pleasing act little by little, day by day, moment by moment. This is the essence of the Christian struggle. Again, this spiritual struggle aims at dispassion; the ontological goal, of course, is the Kingdom.

Catherine Roth, in her introduction to St John Chrysostom's treatise, *On Marriage and Family*, writes:

> Marriage, like monasticism, is a sign of God's kingdom, because it begins to restore the unity of mankind (and the cosmos as a whole) which has been broken up by sin. Thus marriage is both a great mystery in itself and represents a greater mystery, the unity of redeemed mankind in Christ.[146]

Monogamy and fidelity are Godlike characteristics which we are all called to imitate – not only for the sake of others, but for our salvation in Christ the Bridegroom. By God's grace we must flee our paramours, mistresses, and Passions – daily, hourly, moment by moment – so that we may enter the Banquet clothed in a wedding garment suitable for the King. This struggle is essential if we are to be found at the Marriage Feast of the Lamb.

---

[146] Saint John Chrysostom, *On Marriage and Family Life*, trans. Catherine Roth and David Anderson (Crestwood, New York: St. Vladimir's Seminary Press, 1997), p. 10.

Fr Joseph David Huneycutt

Transformation: *On Repentance*

> *The power of the inherited condition of fallenness is not easily overcome, even with the best of intentions. We frequently sin and slip off the path of God-likeness. Because of this distortion of human existence on both the personal and social levels, the spiritual life requires, as well, a* **constant and unceasing repentance.**
>
> *Repentance is the reorientation of our minds, hearts, values, interests, and concerns toward God. Not only do our sins draw us away from the spiritual life, but the very influence of the fallen world creates an atmosphere that disorients our values, decisions, and manner of living. Consequently, repentance is not an occasional spiritual practice, but a constant stance of mind, perpetually reorienting life God-ward.*
>
> *The spiritual life consists in large part in the recognition of and implementation of the* **struggle against the passions.**[147]

Repentance, while often brought about through Confession, does not begin with Confession. As has already been mentioned, like the Prodigal, we "come to our selves" and vow to make amends. We move back toward a right relationship with God in preparing for our Confession; we receive grace and strength in the act of

---

[147] Stanley Samuel Harakas, *Living the Faith: the Praxis of Eastern Orthodox Ethics* (Minneapolis: Light and Life Publishing Company, 1992), p. 88.

confessing. We take the counsel of the priest as witness, trusting in the Holy Spirit. And from there, we go back into the world lightened by the Mystery, fortified by Grace. This whole process is part of Repentance.

We should not, however, understand Repentance as merely rummaging around in our personal sins, engaging in self-flagellation, and trying to uncover and expose as much inner evil, dirt and darkness as possible. Even the devil can help you dig up dirt on yourself! Rather, true repentance is more connected with light than darkness, with the awesome mystery of God's mercy more so than with our dark and evil deeds.

To truly repent, we must turn from the darkness to the light. This is especially done when we recognize God's mercy and forgiveness – and how truly unworthy we are! When standing before God as He truly is, we weep at our shabby and unworthy selves. This brings about amendment of life, new life, through His Son, Christ our Lord. Following this, true repentance is reflected more in our deeds than in our thoughts or words. True repentance is born in our putting off the old self-centered man and putting on the new man in Christ. This bears fruit in our helping our neighbor. Yet, **without** the reconciling sacrament of Confession we are often unable to receive the holy strengthening – and cleansing – necessary to carry out our high calling as Christians.

On Confession

> *A brother asked abba Sisoes, saying, "What shall I do, abba, for I have fallen?" The old man answered, "Get up again." The brother says, "I got up and I fell again." The old man continued, "Get up again and again." The brother asked, "Till when?" The old man answered, "Until you have been seized either by virtue or by sin."*[148]

The thing about Confession is that it is natural. That is, it is Real. Almost everything else we do with our sin is false and unnatural. We punish ourselves, justify our actions, and hide. Yet, in Confession – in opening ourselves to God the Light – we expose the hypocrisy of our double life. In truth, we have been living a lie. Without Confession, Absolution, and Reconciliation we live a lie before God and Man as if it were Reality. In reality, no one is fooled – not our neighbor, not ourselves. And, let's be real, certainly not God.

> The Divine Scripture says: *God said to Adam: Adam, where art thou?* (Gen. 3:9). Why did the Creator of all things say this? Of course, it was in order to dispose Adam to come to his senses, to acknowledge his sin and repent. This is why He said, "Adam, where art thou?" As it were, He said, "Adam, enter into yourself, acknowledge your nakedness and understand what a garment and what a glory you have lost. Adam where are

---

[148] SDECE, p. 72.

you?" In a certain way, as it were, He awakens him and says: "O Adam, come to yourself and confess with humility your sin. Come out of the place where you are hiding. Do you think to hide yourself from Me? Say: 'I have sinned.'"[149]

And thus, each one of us, no matter what transgression he might have fallen into – let him not accuse Adam, but let him reproach himself. And let him show true and worthy repentance like Adam, if he desires to be vouchsafed the Kingdom of Heaven.[150]

The sacrament of Confession is not simply a formal absolution, as if God were angry and demanded expiation. It is something more. It is a part of the therapeutic treatment, the healing of the soul.[151] The Confessor must make it clear that while he certainly stands against the Penitent's sin, he nevertheless stands with him as a person, a fellow struggler.

Thus, having come to oneself and then proceeded on toward repentance through reconciliation, the next step in the process is Communion. The goal is theosis.[152] It is a life-long process that involves:

---

[149] TFCM, p. 108.

[150] TFCM, p. 118.

[151] Cf. OP, p. 17; pp. 23-27.

[152] **THEOSIS:** Connected with the theoria of uncreated Light, theosis, or divinization, is a participation in the uncreated grace of God. At this stage of perfection, one has reached dispassion. Through the cooperation of God with man, theosis is attained through the action of the transfigurative grace of God.

1) Coming to oneself
2) Confession
3) Communion

"Communion," which basically means "common union" with God and mankind, is impossible without first gaining self-knowledge and then ridding oneself continually of sins and passions through Confession. Communion is never fully completed in this life – neither are the first two steps: (1) coming to oneself and (2) repentance. Rather, this is the lifelong path that one treads toward deification, theosis. In this earthly life, we never "graduate." Yet, with God's help, we just proceed from "glory to glory" toward His likeness.

Elder Joseph the Hesychast, *Monastic Wisdom* (Florence, Arizona: St. Anthony's Greek Orthodox Monastery, 1998), p. 409.

Fr Joseph David Huneycutt

Who, What, When, How, and Why

WHO: Confess to your spiritual father. That usually means, in our current situation in America, confessing to your parish priest. With his blessing, you may also confess to another priest and/or establish a relationship with a spiritual father or mother. As with any discipline, consistency in Confession and spiritual direction is important. In other words, lacking grave reason, don't hop around.

WHAT: Confess your sins; do not confess your neighbor's, spouse's, children's, priest's, or bishop's sins. Confess *your* sins. Confession should not be confused with counseling. Both have a God-pleasing place in spiritual health, yet they are not the same thing. However, as with counseling, within Confession there is present: Presenting Problems, Underlying Issues, and Basic Causes. The final category, Basic Causes, may be seen as representative of the Passions. As when we go to a physician and complain of our symptoms, and the physician diagnoses and labels our malady; often in Confession we spout our ill-conceived notions and actions and the Confessor helps us to see the real causes of our behavior. This is necessary for healing to occur.

> For Adam was deceived and truly thought that God did not know about his sin, saying to himself as it were: "I will say that I am naked. God, not knowing the reason for this, will ask, 'How did you become naked?' And I will reply to him, 'I do not know.' Thus I will deceive Him and again receive this, at least He will not

banish me now from Paradise and will not send me to a different place." This is what Adam thought, as now also many people think – and first of all myself – when we hide our sins.[153]

WHEN: Your priest, parish, diocese or jurisdiction, may have a set "rule" of frequency for Confession (in conjunction with frequency of Communion). Ask. Otherwise, essentially: Confess when you need to.

HOW: Although there are local, jurisdictional, and cultural norms, there is no one set form or protocol for Confession. Preparatory prayers and Absolution are normally said in the church in front of an icon and/or the Cross and the Gospel; yet, priests often hear Confessions in their office.

Many people make their Confession in the church prior to, during, or after a service. In Russian practice there is usually a stand, adorned with the Gospel and Cross, before which the Confession is heard by the priest (who serves as witness). Greek practice varies – but it is common to hear Confessions in front of an icon by the iconostasis. For most, these are the norms. However, as is usually the case, there's some wiggle room....

> And so having a time and place established for sacred confession – the time being in the morning*, the place being mainly the Church, or as occasion demands, a modest house, clean and

---

[153] TFCM, p. 109.

peaceful, as Symeon of Thessaloniki says, in which there also must be an icon of our Master Christ, and certainly His Crucifixion – you bring the one to confess there.[154]

WHY: Just as Adam and Eve, after their transgression, were expelled from Paradise lest they ate of the Tree of Life and thus remained forever estranged from God; we, too, by our own sins, estrange ourselves from the Good God. In order to approach the Chalice of the Blood of Him who hung on the Tree of Life, Christ our God, we must first be cleansed.

You cannot drink the cup of the Lord and the cup of demons. You cannot partake

---

[154] Saint Nicodemos the Hagiorite, *Exomolegetarion - A Manual of Confession*, trans. Fr George Dokos (Thessalonica, Greece: Uncut Mountain Press), p. 137.

*Although all times are suitable for confession (especially in time of need), according to Job in his *Concerning the Mysteries*, the most suitable time is in the morning, because at that time, the intellect, of both the Spiritual Father and the penitent, is more clear and collected. That which David says also bears witness to this: "In the morning I slew all the sinners of the land, utterly to destroy out of the city of the Lord all them that work iniquity" (Ps. 100:9), namely, in the morning I killed through confession all those evil thoughts of my heart and destroyed from my soul all the lawless demons and passions. According to Timothy (Canon 18), some should start confessing from ten years old, others from an older age. According to Balsamon, children should confess after six years of age (Responsa ad Interrogationes Marci, Question 48, PG 138, 996C - 997A).

of the table of the Lord and the table of demons (1 Cor. 10:21).

Whoever, therefore, eats the bread or drinks the cup of the Lord in an unworthy manner will be guilty of profaning the body and blood of the Lord. Let a man examine himself, and so eat of the bread and drink of the cup (1 Cor. 11:27-28).

Preparing with the Passions

It is often unnerving to discover just what constitutes our sins. Some of our misdeeds, thoughts, and actions can seem so mundane and natural. Yet upon further inspection we realize that they represent a real hindrance toward reconciliation. We know that, ultimately, the cause of all our sins is disobedience. The Passions may certainly be viewed as basic causes; the following list reveals some of the manifestations of the underlying issues and presenting problems of our struggle toward transformation.[155] It is provided here as an aid toward preparing a good Confession.

PRIDE is manifest in the following ways ...

Irreverence. Deliberate neglect of the worship of God every Sunday in his Church, or being content with a perfunctory participation in it. Disregard of other Holy Days or of additional opportunities for giving God honor. Failure to thank God or to express our gratitude adequately.

Disrespect for God or holy things by deliberately treating them, in thought, word or deed, in a profane, contemptuous or overly familiar manner. Use of holy things for personal advantage, or the attempt to bribe or placate God by religious practices or promises.

---

[155] Taken from *Saint Augustine's Prayer Book* (West Park, New York: Holy Cross Publications, 1967, revised), pp. 112-121. Used by permission.

Sentimentality. Being satisfied with pious feelings and beautiful ceremonies without striving to obey God's will.

Presumption. Dependence on self rather than on God, with the consequent neglect of the means of grace – sacraments and prayer. Dispensation of ourselves from ordinary duties on the grounds that we are superior persons. Satisfaction or complacency over our spiritual achievements. Refusal to avoid, when possible, immediate occasions of temptation. Preference for our own ideas, customs, schemes or techniques. Foolish optimism.

Failure to recognize our job as a divine vocation or to offer our work to God. Unwillingness to surrender to and abide in Christ, to let him act in and through us. Failure to offer to God regularly in intercession the persons or causes that have or should enlist our interest and support.

Distrust. Refusal to recognize God's wisdom, providence, and love. Worry, anxiety, misgivings, scrupulosity, or perfectionism. Attempts to discern or control the future by spiritualism, astrology, fortune-telling, or the like. Magic or superstition.

Over-sensitiveness. Expectation that others will dislike, reject or mistreat us; over-readiness so to interpret their attitude, or quickness to take offense. Unfounded suspicions.

Timidity in accepting responsibility, or cowardice in facing difficulty or suffering. Surrender to feelings of depression, gloom, pessimism, discouragement, self-pity, or fear of death, instead of fighting to be brave, cheerful and hopeful.

Disobedience. Rejection of God's known will in favor of our own interests or pleasures. Disobedience of the legitimate (and therefore divinely ordained) laws, regulations, or authority of the Church, state, husband, parents, teachers, etc.; or slow and reluctant obedience. Failure when in authority to fulfil responsibilities or to consider the best interests of those under us.

Refusal to learn God's nature or will as revealed in Scripture, expounded in instructions or expert advice, or discernible through prayer, meditation, or the reading of religious books. Absorption in our own affairs, leaving little time, energy, or interest for the things of God.

Violation of Confidence. Breaking of legitimate promises or contracts. Irresponsibility. Treachery. Unnecessary disappointment of another, or the causing of shame or anxiety to those who love us.

Impenitence. Refusal to search out and face up to our sins, or to confess and admit them before God. Disregard of our sins or pretense that we are better than we are. Self-justification or discounting our sins as insignificant, natural, or inevitable. Self-righteous comparison of ourselves with others.

Refusal to accept just punishment or to make due reparation when possible. Deceit or lying to escape the consequences of our sins, or allowing another to suffer the blame for our faults. Overcompensation or attempts at self-reform or self-vengeance, to avoid surrender to God in humble penitence.

Shame (hurt pride), sorrow for ourselves because our sins make us less respectable than we like to think we are, or because we fear punishment of injury to our reputation, rather than sorrow for what sin is in the eyes of God. Refusal to admit we were in the wrong or to apologize. Refusal to accept forgiveness from God or others. Doubt that God can forgive our sins, or failure to use the means of getting assurance of His forgiveness when we need it. Unwillingness to forgive ourselves.

Vanity. Crediting to ourselves rather than to God our talents, abilities, insights, accomplishments, good works. Refusal to admit indebtedness to others, or adequately to express gratitude for their help. Hypocrisy. Pretense to virtues we do not posses. False humility. Harsh judgments on others for the faults we excuse in ourselves.

Boasting, exaggeration, drawing attention to ourselves by talking too much, by claiming ability, wisdom, experience or influence that we do not have, or by eccentric or ostentatious behavior. Undue concern over, or expenditure of time, money, or energy on looks, dress, surroundings, etc., in order to impress others; or deliberate slovenliness for the same purpose. Seeking, desiring, or relishing flattery or compliments.

Arrogance. Insisting that others conform to our wishes, recognize our leadership, accept our own estimate of our worth. Being overbearing, argumentative, opinionated, obstinate.

Snobbery. Pride about race, family, position, personality, education, skill, achievements, or possessions.

ANGER is manifest in the following ways ...

Resentment. Refusal to discern, accept or fulfill God's vocation. Dissatisfaction with the talents, abilities, or opportunities He has given us. Unwillingness to face up to difficulties or sacrifices. Unjustified rebellion or complaint at the circumstances of our lives. Escape from reality or the attempt to force our will upon it. Transference to God, to our parents, to society, or to other individuals of the blame for our maladjustment; hatred of God or antisocial behavior. Cynicism. Annoyance at the contrariness of things: profanity or grumbling.

Pugnacity. Attack upon another in anger. Murder in deed or desire. Combativeness or nursing of grudges. Injury to another by striking, cursing, or insulting him; or by damaging his reputation or property. Quarrelsomeness, bickering, contradiction, nagging, rudeness, or snubbing.

Retaliation. Vengeance for wrongs real or imagined, or the plotting thereof. Hostility, sullenness, or rash judgment. Refusal to forgive or to offer or accept reconciliation. Unwillingness to love, to do good to, or to pray for enemies. Boycotting or ostracizing another for selfish reasons. Spoiling others' pleasure by uncooperativeness or disdain, because we have not got our way, or because we feel out of sorts or superior.

LUST is manifest in the following ways ...

Unchastity. Violation of the Church's marriage laws. Lack of consideration for one's partner in the use of the marital relationship. Refusal to fulfill the purpose of Holy Matrimony in the bringing forth and giving adequate care to children, or to take our full share in responsibilities or work involved. Unfaithfulness to one's spouse. Sexual indulgence outside of matrimony, in thought or act, alone or with others.

Immodesty. Stimulation of sexual desire in others by word, dress or action; or in oneself by reading, pictures, or fantasies. Collecting or recounting dirty stories.

Prudery. Fear of sex or condemnation of it as evil in itself. Refusal to seek adequate sexual instruction or the attempt to prevent others from obtaining it. Stimulation of excessive and harmful curiosity by undue secrecy. Repression of sex.

ENVY is manifest in the following ways ...

Jealousy. Offense at the talents, success, or good fortune of others. Selfish or unnecessary rivalry or competition. Pleasure at others' difficulties or distress. Belittling others.

Malice. Ill-will, false accusations, slander, backbiting. Reading false motives into others' behavior. Initiation, collection, or retelling gossip. Arousing, fostering, or organizing antagonism against others. Unnecessary criticism, even when true. Deliberate annoyance of others, teasing or bullying.

Contempt. Scorn of another's virtue, ability, shortcomings, or failings. Prejudice against those we consider inferior, or who consider us inferior, or who seem to threaten our security or position. Ridicule of persons, institutions, or ideals.

GLUTTONY is manifest in the following ways...

Intemperance. Overindulgence in food, drink, smoking, or other physical pleasures. Fastidiousness, fussiness, demanding excessively high standards, or dilettantism. Condemnation of some material things or pleasures as evil in themselves, attempting to prohibit their use rather than their abuse.

Lack of Discipline. Negligence in keeping the days of fasting or abstinence, or failure to use other needed means of self-discipline. Neglect of bodily health – not getting sufficient rest, recreation, exercise, or wholesome nourishment. Failure to use or to cooperate with available medical care when ill. Use of sickness as a means of escape from responsibilities.

COVETOUSNESS [AVARICE] is manifest in the following ways ...

Inordinate Ambition. Pursuit of status, power, influence, reputation, or possessions at the expense of the moral law, or other obligations, or of the rights of others. Ruthless or unfair competition. Putting self or family first. Conformity to standards we recognize as wrong or inadequate in order to get ahead. Intrigue or conspiracy for self-advancement.

Domination. Seeking to use or possess others. Overprotection of children; refusal to correct or punish lest we lose their affection; insistence that they conform to our ideal for them contrary to their own vocation. Imposing our will on others by force, guile, whining, or refusal to cooperate. Over-readiness to advise or command; abuse of authority. Patronizing, pauperizing, putting others under a debt of gratitude, or considering ourselves ill-used when others' affection or compliance is not for sale.

Respect for persons, favoritism, partiality, flattery, fawning, or bribery to win support or affection. Refusal to uphold the truth to fulfill duties, to perform good acts, or to defend those wrongfully attacked, because we fear criticism or ridicule, or because we seek to gain the favor or approval or others. Leading, tempting, or encouraging others to sin.

Prodigality. Waste of natural resources or personal possessions. Extravagance or living beyond our income, to impress others or to maintain status. Failure to pay debts. Gambling more than we can afford to lose, or to win unearned profits. Unnecessary borrowing or carelessness with others' money. Expenditure on self of what is needed for the welfare of others.

Penuriousness. Undue protection of wealth or security. Selfish insistence on vested interests or on claimed rights. Refusal to support or help those who have a claim on us. Sponging on others. Stinginess. Failure to give due proportion of our income to Church and charity, or of our time and energy to good works. Failure to pay pledges promised to the Church or charities, when able to do so.

SLOTH is manifest in the following ways ...

Laziness. Indolence in performing spiritual, mental, or physical duties, or neglect of family, business, or social obligations or courtesies. Procrastination of disliked tasks. Busyness or triviality to avoid more important commitments. Devotion of excessive time to rest, recreations, amusement, television, light reading, or the like. Waste of employer's time, or shoddy or inadequate work.

Indifference. Unconcern over injustice to others, especially that caused by currently accepted social standards; or unmindfulness of the suffering of the world. Failure to become adequately informed on both sides of contemporary issues or on the Christian principles involved. Neglect of duties to state or community. Failure to provide adequately for, or to treat justly those in our employ.

Ignoring of needy, lonely, or unpopular persons in our own or the parish family, or in the neighborhood; or unwillingness to minister to them. Insufficient attention to the religious and other needs of our family. Failure to fulfill our obligation of Christian missionary witness, or to take a full and informal part in the effort to make the Church's unity and holiness a manifest reality on earth.

In preparing for Confession, insight into our motivations and solutions for the same may become apparent. It often happens that the penitent is granted insight into the sinful actions – and even a God-pleasing remedy and course of action – while in the act of Confession. Yet it is *after* the Confession when the real work begins.

> Namely, first oppose the passion, then hate it, and finally practice the particular virtue opposed to it, doing all this, if we

can so say — in an atmosphere of prayer.[156]

As to things, which you are sure are acceptable to God, such as virtues, you should seek them and ask for them only in order to please God more and to serve Him better, and for no other purpose, be it even spiritual.[157]

Virtues are performed through assiduity and attention; they are acquired through our battles and toils, while the spiritual [gifts] are … accorded by Christ to those who struggle. For example, fasting and chastity are virtues, because they make pleasure wither and hold the fires of the body in check. They are the work of our free will and decision. But to practice these virtues without difficulty and to arrive at purity and perfect impassibility is the highest gift of God. On the contrary, to rule over irascibility and nascent anger is a great struggle, no moderate toil. But to arrive at the point where one experiences no commotion from them and one possesses serenity of heart and perfect mildness is the work of God alone.[158]

---

[156] UW, p. 114.
[157] UW, p. 201.
[158] SDECE, p. 129.

SEQUE

Planting, Nurturing, and Reaping

Do not be deceived ... whatever a man sows, that he will also reap. For he who sows to his own flesh will from the flesh reap corruption; but he who sows to the Spirit will from the Spirit reap eternal life (Gal. 6:7-8).

The story is told of the novice who approached his spiritual father stating that he wished to learn obedience. The elder handed him a dry stick and told him to take it to the top of a hill, push it into the ground, and water each and every day for a year. At the end of the 365 days, the young novice was instructed to return to the elder and relate his progress.

The novice did as he was told and dutifully watered the stick every day for a year. After the year was completed, he again visited the spiritual elder. The elder asked him what happened. The novice said, "Nothing! Absolutely nothing happened! I did as you said, every day – for the entire year – I watered that old stick and nothing happened!" To which the elder replied: "Sure it did! Something happened! You learned obedience!"

Obedience, like all virtue, is its own reward. The saying bears repeating: Obedience is its own reward. Yet there is no reward, only sorrow is reaped, when we allow transgressions – Passions – to be sown in our souls. We foster this unwanted growth, the Passions, when we allow sin to become habit. We must, instead, foster Virtue by practicing good habits and, cooperating with God's grace, overcoming the bad. The nurture of this virtuous and God-pleasing garden is accomplished through godly labor, the struggle – or ascesis.

We can say briefly that to practice
asceticism is to apply God's law, to keep
His commandments. The effort which
we make to subordinate the will of man
to the will of God, and to be changed by
this, is called ascesis.[159]

Ascetic disciplines are nothing more than
the means to mortify the old Adam and
crucify our will, our passions, and the
desires that work in us for iniquity.
Ascesis is only a way of showing our love
and tender feelings toward God.[160]

This godly struggle, ascesis, may serve as both a
catalyst toward and the fruit of Confession. We offer to
God that which we have. Sometimes, what we have is
awful, diseased, and sinful. This we offer to God in
Confession; the more of this disease that is purged, the
more we are cleansed by grace to receive the gifts of the
Holy Spirit.

The point is this: he who sows sparingly
will also reap sparingly, and he who sows
bountifully will also reap bountifully (2
Cor. 9:6).

As was stated in the first chapter, the purpose of
this book is to educate and encourage Christians in the

---

[159] OP, p. 47.
[160] Father Matta El-Meskeen (Matthew the Poor), *Orthodox Prayer Life – The Interior Way* (Crestwood, New York: St. Vladimir's Seminary Press, 2003), p. 118.

struggles of spiritual warfare according to the teachings of the Church Fathers and contemporary theologians within a creative format – using the Two Trees as found in the Book of Genesis. While the ultimate goal is salvation, the immediate purpose is repentance – including making a good Confession.

The Meditations which follow in Part Two were designed to assist in the reflective process necessary in preparing for Confession and thereby reaping the good things which God has in store for those who love him.

> Therefore, as in the beginning Adam in Paradise was free and sinless, and by his free will obeyed the enemy, was deceived and transgressed the commandment of God – so on the contrary we, being regenerated by holy Baptism, delivered from slavery and becoming free, if we do not obey by our own free will our enemy the devil, this cunning one will in no way be able to place in us any kind of evil.[161]

---

[161] TFCM, p. 117.

Fr Joseph David Huneycutt

PART TWO

About the Meditations

The following presentations, or Meditations, are designed to educate, encourage, and lead one, or many, to a better understanding of the struggles of spiritual warfare and toward a good Confession.

All of the Mediations in this section are original and have been used, in some form or another, within retreats, workshops, and other presentations. On occasion, especially during a two-day event, I have also read from pertinent presentations by other authors. One Meditation that has proven very helpful in preparing for Confession is "Bless My Enemies, O Lord," by St Nikolai Velimirovich (included in Appendix V).

The first Meditation is on the Prayer of St Ephraim the Syrian. This prayer, written by St Ephraim in the 4th century, is a regular part of the Orthodox Christian's prayer "diet" during the Great Fast of Lent. It may also be said throughout the year as part of one's prayer rule.

Next is a presentation about the nature of sin, the repetitiveness and habits of sin, and our longing for God. This talk is based, primarily, on Flannery O'Conner's short story, *The Peeler*. It is a reflection on our struggle – both in avoiding God and longing to return to Him.

The story of a little boy named "Andrew" developed from a sermon I once heard preached by the Rev'd Andrew Sloane (hence the title). I am indebted to him for this simple story of "Yay and Uh-Oh," transgression and reconciliation. Andrew works well with children and adults.

The Wait is about transformation. There are elements of the Meditation that have been gleaned from the writings of C.S. Lewis and others. The main point is that we should be aware of our own transgressions and not judge others. God sees things differently than we. We must struggle to see God – Christ – in others.

The final presentation, *The Two Trees*, has its own introduction. Much of the effectiveness of this story is in the delivery. Although a cryptic tale of spiritual struggle, it often serves as the highpoint of reflection and insight during retreats.

The Great Prayer of St Ephraim the Syrian and the Moral Person

O Lord and Master of my life,
Take from me the spirit of sloth, despair,
lust of power, and idle talk;
But give rather the spirit of chastity, humility,
patience, and love to Thy servant.
Yea, O Lord and King, grant me to see my
own transgressions and not to judge
my brother, for blessed art Thou unto ages of
ages. Amen.[162]

The first part of the Prayer bids God, the "Lord and Master of [our] life," to take certain "spirits" from us; then follows a petition for the Lord to give certain "spirits". The Prayer concludes by bidding the Master to grant sight and self judgment. Thus, we bid God to take, give, and grant. Underlying the petitions of the Prayer are several admissions. The first admission is that we have a Master, who is God. We come face to face with the God of the living at the outset of the Prayer.

In beseeching the Lord to take certain things from us, we are admitting that we currently possess them. The first spirit to be removed is "sloth."[163] Whether the ascetic

---

[162] Although the Prayer was originally written in Syriac, I have defined the terms by use of the Greek text merely as a matter of clarification, because various English translations exist. The Greek translation is taken from *Greek Orthodox Holy Week and Easter Services*, comp. George L. Papadeas (Daytona Beach, Florida: Patmos Press, 1994), p. 107.

[163] αργιας (αργος): inactive, unemployed; idle, adverse from labor; unprofitable, hollow; to be unemployed, to be inoperative,

exercise is prayer, fasting, or almsgiving, sloth leads to an abundance of sins. This has been true in all ages. However, it seems that sloth is currently viewed as the means and end of the modern person. What would the Lord ask of those who sit idly in front of the TV for hours on end? Or, how about our sloth in areas of charity, hospitality, prayer and good works? Thus, we must begin by asking God to deliver us from this spirit of sloth in order to practice good works, watchfulness, and vigilance. St Mark the Ascetic warns us of three giants: spiritual ignorance, forgetfulness, and laziness. He claims that if these three are slain "all other powers of the evil spirits are removed."[164] It must be added, however, that a person might be extremely busy, productive, and active – all the while neglecting the things that are needful. This is also a form of sloth.

The next spirit is variously translated as "despair" or "meddling."[165] What do despair and meddling have to do with each other? Despair is often the result of failed pride. And what causes most meddling? Pride and the belittling spirit of superiority. It should go without saying that these never cease to fail us in the moral life.

> Besides that, they learn to be idlers, gadding about from house to house, and not only idlers, but gossipers and busybodies, saying what they should not (1 Tim. 5:13).

---

to linger. NB: All definitions of Greek terms are taken from *The Analytical Greek Lexicon Revised*, ed. Harold K. Mouton (Grand Rapids: Zondervan, 1978).

[164] OP, p. 255.

[165] περιεργίας (περιεγος): over-careful; officious, a busybody.

We should, rather, strive for hope and joy. This is the goal of the spiritually moral person. Despair is of the devil.

> St Symeon the New Theologian, an experienced spiritual physician, recognized that long and untimely sorrowing of the heart 'darkens and disturbs the mind,' it banishes pure prayer and compunction from the soul and creates a painful pining of the heart which results in hardness and painful callousness. This is how the demons bring about despair.[166]

In admitting the defeating sin of despair and meddling, we are able to open our eyes to the Sovereign Lord of Hope and Joy. Note the words of St Paul:

> Finally, brethren, whatever things are true, whatever things are noble, whatever things are just, whatever things are pure, whatever things are lovely, whatever things are of good report, if there is any virtue and if there is anything praise-worthy – meditate on these things (Phil. 4:8).

How can we avoid the "lust of power"[167] when our culture makes of it a supreme goal? This moral self-

---

[166] OP, p. 179.

[167] φιλαρχιας (φιλ - αρχη, αρχω, αρχων): first place, headship; high estate, eminence; authority; a principality, prince, of spiritual existence; to be first; to govern; one invested with power and dignity, chief, ruler, magistrate.

love is advertised by our media and taught by our culture to such an extent that it seems archaic to criticize it.

> But Jesus called them to him and said, "You know that the rulers of the Gentiles lord it over them, and their great men exercise authority over them" (Mt. 20:25).

What of the moral person?

> It shall not be so among you; but whoever would be great among you must be your servant, and whoever would be first among you must be your slave; even as the Son of man came not to be served but to serve, and to give his life as a ransom for many (Mt. 20:26-27).

It is our high calling to be servants to our fellows and slaves to God. Allowing God to be our Lord and Master is a humbling experience.

The next section of the Prayer should cause fear and trembling for us all. Here we ask the Lord to take from us the spirit of "idle talk."[168] Here we connect our tongue with the sin of sloth.

> I tell you, on the day of judgment men will render account for every careless word they utter; for by your words you will be justified, and by your words you will be condemned (Mt. 12:36) .

---

[168] αργολογιας (αργο - λογιας): idle talk.

Instead, giving in to the spirit of idle talk, we speak to make ourselves look better, which leads us to be judgmental and slanderous. We live in an age of unprecedented, unbridled, unadulterated idle talk. The modern person fills the hours with radio, television, phone, internet, and gossip. The moral person should practice self-criticism, examination of conscience, and silence.

We now come to the second part of St Ephraim's prayer wherein we ask the Lord and Master to give us certain "spirits". The first gift besought is "chastity".[169] Chastity is synonymous with faithfulness. It is self-control, whole-mindedness, and the opposite of a broken character – which is caused by the sin of sloth.

> Bid the older men to be temperate, serious, sensible, sound in faith, in love, and in steadfastness (Tit. 2:2). Yet woman will be saved through bearing children, if she continues in faith and love and holiness, with modesty (1 Tim. 2:15).

By these examples from Scripture, we can see that the meaning of chastity is more than fidelity. It is fidelity to the Truth. Truth is a Person, Jesus Christ. Thus to be chaste, we must be in a relationship where we keep our hearts and minds on Christ. This fidelity is required in the moral Christian life.

The second gift is "humility".[170] In contrast to Greek literature where humility is viewed as a weakness,

---

[169] σωφροσυνης (σωφρωη, σωφροσυνη): sanity, soundness of mind, a sane mind; female modesty.

[170] ταπεινοφροσυνης (ταπεινοφρων, ταπεινοφροσυνη): humble-minded; lowliness or humility of mind and deportment, modesty.

Scripture celebrates it as a cardinal virtue.[171] However, as with Greek literature, this virtue is missing from the paradigm of modern man. Rather, it is the model of the Savior: "And being found in the human form he humbled himself and became obedient unto death, even death on a cross" (Phil. 2:8). It is our calling as Christians.

> Finally, all of you, have unity of spirit, sympathy, love of the brethren, a tender heart and a humble mind (1 Pet. 3:8) ... serving the Lord with all humility and with tears and with trials which befell me through the plots of the Jews (Acts 20:19)... with all lowliness and meekness, with patience, forbearing one another in love, eager to maintain the unity of the Spirit in the bond of peace (Eph. 4:2). Do nothing from selfishness or conceit, but in humility count others better than yourselves (Phil. 2:3).

Our society views pride as a virtue. Yet pride is residual of the fall of Lucifer and his angels from the heavenly realm. As Vlachos writes, "Of course when a person's heart has been purified, he must not be proud of it, for no creatures are purer than the bodiless ones, the angels, and yet Lucifer, by exalting himself, became the devil and is unclean.[172] The enemy of souls is pride incarnate. The opposite of pride – humility – is the very essence of the Holy Incarnation.

---

[171] Jeffrey, p. 366.
[172] OP, p. 200.

The discipline of the moral person requires "patience".[173] Yet, it is inherent in our fallen nature to be impatient, quick to judge and condemn.

> By your endurance you will gain your lives (Lk. 21:19). More than that, we rejoice in our sufferings, knowing that suffering produces endurance, and endurance produces character, and character produces hope, and hope does not disappoint us, because God's love has been poured into our hearts through the Holy Spirit which has been given us (Rom. 5:3-5) ... for you know that the testing of your faith produces steadfastness. And let steadfastness have its full effect, that you may be perfect and complete, lacking nothing (Jas. 1:3, 4).

How can we grow in patience, lest God send us trials? The virtue of patience is a great comfort – one rarely praised in our day of quick fixes (e.g., abortion, drugs, euthanasia). The fruit of the moral life is "love."[174] "That is to say, when a person lives naturally, he wants to know God completely, he desires only God, and he struggles to attain God, that is, to attain communion with God. The fruit of this pursuit is love. A person united with God

---

[173] υπομονης (υπομονη, ης; εν υπομονη & δι υπομονης): patient endurance; patient awaiting; a patient frame of mind, patience; perseverance; endurance; constantly, preservingly; an enduring of affliction; the act of suffering; undergoing.
[174] αγαπης (αγαπε, ης): love, generosity, kindly concern, devotedness; love-feasts.

acquires the blessed state of love, since God is love."[175]
Contrast this with what could seemingly be a definition of
our own age:

> These are blemishes on your love feasts,
> as they boldly carouse together, looking
> after themselves; waterless clouds, carried
> along by winds; fruitless trees in late
> autumn, twice dead, uprooted; wild waves
> of the sea, casting up the foam of their
> own shame; wandering stars for whom
> the nether gloom of darkness has been
> reserved for ever (Jude 12-13).

Next, we beseech the Lord and Master to "grant"
us two things: sight[176] and non-judgmentalness.[177] Is there
a difference between the words "give"[178] and "grant?"[179]
We ask God to give us "the spirit of chastity, humility,
patience and love." We then ask Him to grant us "to see
[our] own transgressions and not to judge [our] brother."
Isn't it possible that the difference lies in that with which
we are familiar and that which is foreign to us? For
instance, we are not all that familiar with chastity, humility,
patience, and love. True, we may experience them from
time to time. Yet for most, familiarity with these virtues is

---

[175] OP, p. 250.
[176] οραν (οραω): to see, behold; to mark, observe; to be admitted
to witness [with εον = to reveal one's self, to present one's self].
[177] πταισματα (πταιω): to cause to stumble; to stumble, stagger,
fall; to make a false step; to err, offend, transgress.
[178] give: to make a present of. *Merriam Webster's Collegiate
Dictionary*, 10th edition (Springfield: Merriam-Webster, 1994).
[179] grant: to consent, to carry out for a person, allow fulfillment
of. *Merriam-Webster's Collegiate Dictionary*, 10th edition.

uncommon. On the other hand, we are all too familiar with seeing transgressions and being judgmental! In the Prayer we ask God to transform this very sight and judgment. We ask the master to help us to see our own transgressions and not our brothers'. This last part of the Prayer is essential to our soul's petition for transformation. All that precedes this section mirrors our current state and our needs. However, attainment of this high calling is impossible lest we, with God's help, work out our own salvation with fear and trembling (Phil 2:12) – judging, not our brother, but ourselves.

> Jesus looked up and said to her, "Woman, where are they? Has no one condemned you? Neither do I condemn you" (Jn. 8:10, 11).

The cornerstone of the Prayer of St Ephraim is relationship: "O Lord and Master of my life." Unlike the "individual," who is self-centric, a "person" is someone who is in relationship in this case, to the Lord Jesus Christ. From the outset of the Prayer, we are turning over our lives to the One who is to be at the center of our life, Jesus Christ. By our very words (in the Prayer) we invite discipline and imply obedience, both of which are missing in the self-centered modern person.

> To humble oneself before God is to admit one's weakness and dependence, God's power and goodness, and one's trust and hope in God. This disposition (described in Mic. 6:8 as one of the principle requirements of a "good" life) is expressed in obedience and repentance

(James 4:6-10). Such humility is a chief characteristic of the OT heroes of faith (e.g., Gideon, Hannah, David, and Solomon) and a virtue celebrated repeatedly in wisdom literature.[180]

The other key to the Prayer is sight. We pray that God will grant us to see our own transgressions. This is a plea for our own salvation. How can we continually see the demons in those around us when our own passions condemn us?

> Why do you see the speck in your brother's eye, but do not notice the log that is in your own eye? Or how can you say to your brother, "Let me take the speck out of your eye," when there is a log in your own eye? You hypocrite, first take the log out of your own eye, and then you will see clearly to take the speck out of your brother's eye (Mt. 7:3-5).

Our eyes are filled with the modern "judges" of the media: news anchors, politicians, talk show hosts, and all the other "talking heads" of the air waves. The moral person must guard against the promiscuous judgments spewed forth daily from the media.

> The lamp of the body is the eye. If therefore your eye is good, your whole body will be full of light. But if your eye is bad, your whole body will be full of

---

[180] Jeffrey, p. 366.

darkness, if therefore the light that is in you is darkness, how great is that darkness! No one can serve two masters; for either he will hate the one and love the other, or else he will be loyal to the one and despise the other. You cannot serve God and mammon (Mt. 6:22-24).

No one can serve two masters. Herein lies the key to understanding the Prayer of St Ephraim the Syrian as a moral tool for the Christian life. We pray that God take from us the spirit of the world and give us, rather, His spirit. Within this short prayer lies the essence of our struggle known as spiritual warfare.

Fr Joseph David Huneycutt

The Peeler, the Hound, and the Addict

At present, before the Day of Judgment comes, even though the Spirit cannot dwell within those who are unworthy, He nevertheless is present in a limited way with those who have been baptized, hoping that their conversion will result in salvation.
– St Basil the Great[181]

In Flannery O'Conner's short story, *The Peeler*,[182] the main character, Hazel Motes, is on a journey. It is a spiritual journey which he has confused as a carnal tour. Along the way, he encounters a blind evangelist who sees into his darkened soul.

In the story, Haze happens upon a man hawking potato peelers in downtown Taulkinham. The brown potatoes go into the peeler and come out on the other side, white. (This is key to understanding the story.) At this even, in addition to acquiring a shadow named Enoch Emery, Haze also witnesses the blind man and a young girl who are handing out "Jesus tracts." He makes eye contact with the young girl; overhears her offering to buy a peeler for less money; and ends up buying one with change to spare and running after the blind evangelist and the young girl with peeler in hand and Enoch in tow.

When questioned by Enoch, Haze denies he is following the Jesus freaks. His attraction to them – especially since he wasn't interested in the tract he was given – is puzzling. When the blind man repeatedly accuses Haze of following him, Haze denies it, saying he was following the girl. He gives her the potato peeler. The

---

[181] St. Basil, p. 67.
[182] Flannery O'Connor, *The Complete Stories* (New York: The Noonday Press, 1998), pp. 63-80.

girl acts ungrateful, but the blind man tells her to take the gift. Haze accuses the girl of being a flirt – giving him the "fast eye." She denies it and complains that Haze tore up his Jesus tract.

While this argument continues, the blind man remains convinced that Haze followed them because he was seeking Jesus. "Listen," the blind man said, "you can't run away from Jesus. Jesus is a fact. If you're looking for Jesus, the sound of it will be in your voice." Ignoring Haze's protests, the blind man feels his face, "You got a secret need," the blind man says. "Them that know Jesus once can't escape him in the end."

Haze denies it, saying: "I ain't never known Him." "You got a least knowledge," the blind man says. "That's enough. You know His name and you're marked. If Jesus has marked you there ain't nothing you can do about it. Them that have knowledge can't swap it for ignorance."

"You're marked with knowledge," the blind man says. "You know what sin is and only them that know what it is can commit it. I knew all the time we were walking here somebody was following me," he says. "You couldn't have followed her. Wouldn't anybody follow her. I could feel there was somebody near with an urge for Jesus."

The blind man and the girl continue to try to get Haze to admit his sins, repent, and turn to Jesus. Haze finally jerks his arm away, claiming that he is as clean as they are.

"Fornication," the blind man says. Haze tries to wiggle out of the accusation by claiming that he doesn't believe in sin.

"You do," the blind man says, "you're marked."

"I ain't marked," Haze says, "I'm free."

"You're marked free," the blind man says. "Jesus loves you and you can't escape his mark." He then encourages Haze to help them distribute their Jesus tracts at a theater. Instead, Haze ends up ridiculing them to those exiting the show. He eventually says to himself, "I don't need no Jesus. I got Lenora Watts." He leaves the evangelists and heads toward his woman with his shadow, Enoch Emory, fast on his heels.

On the way, Emory tries to get Haze to visit some prostitutes. Haze declines, claiming he's already got a woman. Emory then shows Haze the peeler that the girl had ended up giving him, the one Haze had bought for her. Needless to say, the two young men end on bad terms.

As Haze enters the woman's house, he reflects on his first time with a woman, just the night before, wherein he was not very successful. As he undresses, he thinks back to when he was twelve years old and wanted to follow his dad and other men into a carnival tent that was forbidden him. He finally convinced the barker to allow him entrance, only to find a mixture of sex and death on display: a nude white woman writhing around in a black-covered casket.

After escaping the carny scene, the next woman he sees is his mother. It is evident to her that her boy has seen something scary, vile. She repeatedly questions him, "What have you seen?" He gives no answer. After hitting him with a stick fails to draw a response, she says, "Jesus died to redeem you."

"I never ast him to," he mutters.

The next day he takes his shoes in secret out into the woods. He never wears them except for revivals and in winter. He takes them out of the box and fills the bottoms of them with stones and small rocks and then puts them back on. He laces them up tight and walks in them through the woods what he knows to be a mile, until he comes to a creek, and then he sits down and takes them off and eases his feet in the wet sand. He thinks, that ought to satisfy Him. Nothing happens. If a stone had fallen, he would have taken it for a sign. After a while he draws his feet out of the sand and lets them dry, and then he puts the shoes on again with the rocks still in them and he walks a half mile back before he takes them off.

Unlike the potato peeler, which rendered brown potatoes white, Haze is learning that life outside of paradise is often complicated by murkiness, grey areas. He cannot help but associate women with sin and death. And, at the same time, he seeks redemption ... all the while participating in sin. Such a vision and activity read like insanity, but reflect life in practice: reality. Who hasn't known similar dilemmas? We often run from repentance, accountability ... God.

Even before we come to accept accountability for our actions, we are often troubled by what one writer, Francis Thompson, termed the *Hound of Heaven.*[183]

I fled Him, down the nights and down the days;
I fled Him, down the arches of the years;
I fled Him, down the labyrinthine ways
Of my own mind; and in the mist of tears
I hid from Him, and under running laughter.

I remember the first time I met with a priest to express my interest in pursuing the priesthood. Breaking the ice, I asked: "So, how did you wind up in those

[183] Francis Thompson (1859-1907), "The Hound of Heaven"; http://www.houndsofheaven.com/thepoem.htm (viewed 6/21/07).

clothes?" "I got tired of running from it," he replied. I just about fell out of my chair! That was exactly the place I was coming from.

Up vistaed hopes I sped;
And shot, precipitated,
Adown Titanic glooms of chasmed fears,
From those strong Feet that followed, followed after.
But with unhurrying chase,
And unperturbèd pace, Deliberate speed, majestic instancy,
They beat - and a Voice beat
More instant than the Feet -
"All things betray thee, who betrayest Me."

All things that are against us – that harm us spiritually – do battle against this "hound" that loves us, pursues us. His pursuit is steady, patient, and relentless. Why do we run from Him?

(For, though I knew His love Who followèd,
Yet I was sore adread
Lest, having Him, I must have naught beside.)

This is the reason: We believe that all that we hold dear will be taken away from us if we succumb to Him. Like Jonah who complained of the Lord's mercy even as it was saving his life in the bottom of the sea, we are ungrateful – wishing to stay in our sickened state rather than sacrifice our worldly "gains." And it will ever be so, this flight from Love, until we heed the voice that's saying:

"Ah, fondest, blindest, weakest,
I am He Whom thou seekest!
Thou dravest love from thee, who dravest Me."

As St Augustine wrote: "For Thou hast formed us for Thyself, and our hearts are restless till they find rest in Thee."[184] We long to fill the emptiness inside with worldly cares and pursuits. Yet, our soul longs for the Lord. That which is lacking is precisely That which pursues us. We resist submission, erroneously believing that in so doing we will be bereft of all when, in reality, it is the All that we need. Our souls thirst for God.

For those who have had the pleasure of working with addicts in recovery, you know that one of the joys of the job is attending Narcotics Anonymous (NA) meetings. At these gatherings, one hears how personal emptiness was saturated with the vices of addiction: alcohol, drugs. Over and over again one also hears of those in recovery talking about how it was really a spiritual crisis. They needed fulfillment, but it was God that was lacking.

Recovery is a lifestyle and relapse is often part of the reality of recovery. Relapse happens. Many a recovering addict has suffered the disappointment of "falling off the wagon" after beginning the recovery process. At the NA meetings they always say, "Keep coming back." Part of the reason that those who relapse are encouraged to keep returning is that the community gatherings are cathartic and healing rooms. Another big reason is this: recovery messes up your using. Sin is no longer as encouraging once you know the Truth.

Isn't that what happened with Hazel Motes (whose name, by the way, indicates a blocked or imperfect vision)? He keeps bumping into Jesus, the Peeler, and it messes up his sinning. Isn't that what keeps the subject of

---

[184] *Nicene and Post-Nicene Fathers of the Christian Church, First Series* (Grand Rapids: Eerdmans, 1988), Volume 1, p. 45.

Francis Thomas's poem running? Isn't that what keeps each of us struggling toward the Kingdom? We're all partial to some sin(s). But once we know Christ we can honestly say, "God done messed up my using."

The Passions are only satisfied in Christ.

Keep coming back.

Fr Joseph David Huneycutt

ANDREW

There once was a boy named Andrew.

Andrew was a very happy child and his parents loved him dearly.

Andrew could run, jump, and play outside – and in any room in the house ...

Except the living room.

There was only one rule in Andrew's home: Thou shalt not play in the living room.

Andrew was a contented child. But, more than anything in the world, he desperately desired to play in the living room.

Every time he passed by the room, he longed to play there. More and more he became obsessed with the idea of playing in the forbidden room.

One day, when his parents were next door visiting the neighbors, Andrew seized the opportunity!

He entered the living room. He ran. He jumped. He flew from chair to sofa and back again. He was having so much fun! He couldn't understand why his mother would never allow him to play in the living room. Why, this was the funnest room in the house!

Then it happened.

Crash!

His mother's favorite vase.

It lay broken – shattered – on the floor.

Andrew stopped playing. Not quite knowing what to do, he quickly swept up the pieces of the broken vase and hid them under the skirting of a chair.

Soon, his parents returned. They sensed something was the matter with little Andrew, but he said everything was fine.

It wasn't long before Andrew stopped playing in the hall, the driveway, and in the den.

He even curbed his play outside.

He stopped running and began to mope. His shoulders began to slump. He did not smile. Andrew was no longer a happy contented young boy.

When his parents would ask him about his sullenness, he would only reply: "Everything's fine."

His eyes would no longer look into the living room with a burning desire, but with a sad and terrible fear. There, under his father's favorite formal chair, were hidden the fragments of his mother's favorite vase.

Weeks went by. Months. Andrew's personality sank deeper and deeper under the weight of his worry.

Then it happened.

One day, as he was moping up the hall, he saw his mother emerge from the dreaded room.

Their eyes met.

He knew … she knew …

He was terrified.

Until he saw her squat down and open her arms wide to him.

Then it happened. The tears poured down his face as he snuggled into his mother's embrace.

"Why?" she asked. "Why did you not tell me?"

He didn't have to say a word. His mother saw the fear and sorrow in his eyes. It was only then that she understood why her little boy had been so melancholy.

And it was then that Andrew first knew the wonders of forgiving love.

We do the same thing, do we not? Like St Paul says, "I do not understand my own action. For I do not do what I want, but I do the very thing I hate." Like Adam and Eve in the Garden, who had one rule, we break the commands of God and try to hide our sins under cover of darkness. We live in fear of being found out. It affects our mood, our relationships with those around us – and our relationship with God. Yet, like Andrew's mother, God longs for us to be freed from the bondage of our broken and sinful lives.

He will embrace us with a mother's love ... if we but let Him.

The Wait

In the end, it was only a dream.

Yet, for an eternal moment I felt as if I were the only person in the universe, floating through a vast darkness – no light, anywhere.

Then, off in the distance, I saw a blinding white light such as I had never seen before.

As I approached the light, I became increasingly aware of all the sinful actions of my life.

But it was more than that. I also became extremely aware of my attitudes, past thoughts, and prejudices – so much so that I wanted to leave my body. I wanted to jump out of this dirty sinful self and into the bright Holy Light....

But I could not.

Instead, I entered the brilliant unknown realm just as I was ...

I was greeted by someone that I perceived to be an angel. Unlike the angels I'd always imagined, this being had no wings, no harp, no baby face. He did not sit on a cloud of white.

However, he was extremely beautiful.

"Welcome," said the angel.

I could not tear my eyes away from the beautiful light that radiated from his face.

Again, "Welcome."

"Hello," I muttered, "where am I?"

He smiled and said "Surely you received and accepted our invitation, or you would not be here. You must know where you are."

"No, no," I said, "please tell me."

"This is the Kingdom of God. All is beauty, all is holy, all is love. Everything – including YOU (my dirty little man) is here because God wills it to be so."

"But I'm not worthy," I sighed.

"Yes. You are right, you're not," he replied.

For the first time since my arrival, I was able to peel my eyes away from his radiant face and scan the holy land. I cannot describe for you this place ... its beauty ... the light. Then suddenly, my eyes glimpsed someone I knew – a sinner from earth! I said to the angel "Surely you must be mistaken. I am not in heaven – for look there, that man is a sinner! I knew him. I doubt he believed in Jesus Christ ... and, as far as I know, he never went to church a day in his life! What is he doing here?"

"He was invited," said the guide. "He came."

For a brief horrifying moment, I saw my own reflection in his beautiful face.

As we traveled along, I saw others that I knew – both sinners and saints. I was very confused – and yet, at the same time, quite overwhelmed. I asked my guide many questions. But his answers all had something to do with "they were invited," "accepted our invitation," or, "because God wills it to be so."

Suddenly, I stopped dead in my tracks. There stood Jack Tyndall. I despised him! Oh, how I hated him!

I turned to the light-filled being and said, "I can't believe he is here! I cannot stand him!"

"But, remember," said the angel, "remember ... once, twice – you prayed for him."

[He's right. Although it almost killed me, I did make it a habit to pray for my enemies.]

"Is that why he's here?!" I whined.

"No – that's how you got in," he said.

My head began to swim with confusion. Sure, I'd prayed for my enemies – but, I surely hadn't prayed that I'd spend eternity with them!

Then, almost like a staged parade, one by one, enemies and scoundrels alike all passed before me. I started yelling at my angelic guide.

"But she's an adulteress! Everyone knew she slept around all over town. She had no morals."

"God invited her," he said. "Everything changed when she accepted our invitation."

"Him! I can't believe this, surely I'm in the wrong place. I mean, that guy cared for nothing but money! He had no faith!"

"In you maybe," replied the angel, "but, in his time he donated much money to the Church and to charitable causes, allowing many to live a better life to the glory of God. You may not have recognized it on earth but, here, we look into one's heart – and his is as big as the moon and filled with the love of God."

By now, I'd started to cry. I saw nothing before me but people I'd hated. Where were the folks that I loved. Where was my wife? My mother? My father? Grandmother? Where were all of my friends who'd died?

Almost on the brink of hysteria, I turned to the glowing creature and pleaded "But, where are my loved ones?"

"Why should they be here?" he asked.

"For me!" I shouted. "Because I love them! They are my family! No, maybe they weren't all perfect – but they were good folks. Please, oh please, tell me where are my loved ones?"

He, too, shed a tear. The light subsided a bit, and he showed me his hands, his feet and side. In an instant, I recognized Him.

In that same moment, I became white as snow – no longer feeling dirty and unworthy.

He said to me, "I, too, know love. And it is my love that has brought you, and these people, to this Kingdom. Many whom you love are here also, but you should know that they are no more loved than these whom you hate. For they are all My family. I am the Judge. My Father has given me the reign of His Kingdom. And as you know, I opened my heart for the love of the world – that those who love Me might inherit eternal life."

He then vanished from my sight ...

... and all those who were before me changed.

No.

I changed.

I saw clearly, for the first time, that these were not my enemies. They were ... my family.

All things became clear ... "God so loved the world ..."

"Jesus died for your sins."

"God's will ..."

"God's invitation ..."

"God."

I became overwhelmed with joy! There was shouting, dancing, music and, spread before me – the family, and all the hosts of heaven – was a great feast surrounding the throne of Light!

But, someone was missing. Where was the guide who'd brought me to the banquet – who had opened my eyes?

Where was the Christ – Who had taught me so much? Where was He who loved me? Where was He Who had died that I might live? He was with me just a moment ago ...

Turning to my neighbor, I asked "Where is He? The Bridegroom?"

He nodded in the direction of the gate through which I had entered – and there stood the Lord Jesus, sadly waiting by the entrance to the Kingdom.

"What's wrong? Why does he stand there so sad?"

I couldn't be sure, dear reader, but I thought I heard him say: "He's waiting for Judas" –

The alarm! "Wha ...?

Oh no! My alarm clock ...

"He's waiting for Ju ..."

Time to get up. The alarm!

"Wait! What?"

I was groggy, trying to hold on to the dream. At first it sounded like he'd said, "Judas."

Judas? I was still half sleeping, but I knew that couldn't be right …

But, as I slammed my hand down upon the snooze button, I heard clearly: "He's waiting on you."

"He's waiting for you."

Fr Joseph David Huneycutt

The Two Trees

This meditation serves as the centerpiece of the Two Trees retreat. Originally titled **The Wilderness***, it is the final presentation before time for Confessions. I have used this cryptic talk in various settings: adult male only, adult female only, mixed adults, mixed teens – and mixed pre-teens. It was the latter group, junior high kids, which surprised me. They were greatly moved, grasping the message even better than their older teen peers. In my experience, the following meditation works best when read aloud with pauses between each of the 33 sections. On some occasions, the Prayer of St Ephraim was inserted between each section, with pregnant pauses before and after. On other occasions, someone inserted the Jesus Prayer: "Lord Jesus Christ, Son of God, have mercy on me a sinner." A simple long pause, 10-15 seconds, is also sufficient. Silence, interspersed throughout this meditation, is necessary for participants to grasp the material. I have placed three crosses [+ + +] between each short section to note where this long silence is most appropriate.*

Let us travel into the Wilderness ...

Ahead, through the blinding haze, nothing appears. All is naught, all is night.

To our left is a garden, an oasis of calm tranquility. It is a beautiful garden. In the middle of the garden stands a tree. A most beautiful tree – tall and strong with abundant fruit.

Ahead is the Wilderness. To our left, the Garden.

When we look opposite the Garden, to the right of the Wilderness, we see a hill, a dark vision of gloom and death.

It is ugly and skull shaped. On the top stands a tree. A most terrifying tree. Bloody, cross shaped.

Our eyes cannot continue to look upon the hill. For a moment, we again look straight ahead into nothing. Then we find our eyes, slowly at first — then in a flash — returning to the beautiful garden. It looks like heaven. For this vision, we are thankful. For the Hill looks like Hell.

+ + +

Again in the Wilderness ...

Our mouths are dry, our bellies empty. What shall we do to quench our thirst? To quell our appetites? To refresh our souls?

We stare into the abundant garden. Our eyes receive a feast, our mouths and bellies cry out, "Yes!" And our soul must follow as our feet move toward the Garden. We are hesitant. Yet, remembering the vision of the Hill, our pace is quickened.

The Garden, though seemingly far away, is under our feet in an instant. (Did we move toward it? Or it toward us?) A stirring in our soul says, "No." Yet, with eager hands and greedy passion, we pluck from the Tree in the Garden. Our bodies are awakened. O fruit of passion ...

+ + +

Again in the Garden ...

The fruit that looked so wonderful, so inviting, eventually turned bitter in our bellies. It appealed to our eyes, tongues, and senses. And although our souls said "No," we listened instead to our bodies. Now, with bellies full, we are still not satisfied.

For once, we understand our soul's definition of the fruits of the Garden's tree: Pride, Anger, Lust, Envy, Gluttony, Avarice, and Sloth ... "Pale Gas." To us, however, it is familiar fruit; the source of our nourishment. It all seems very **natural**.

Even silencing our soul seems familiar ... *natural*.

+ + +

Again in the Garden ...

From where we sit in the Garden we see, off in the distance, the Hill, the Tree, and what appears to be a dying man hanging there. In the Garden, there is light. Yet, as far as we can see, the Hill looks dark and foreboding.

Again, we listen to our soul which seems to long for the Hill. We begin to make our way out of the Garden – toward the Wilderness – only to realize that the headway that we make seems to take forever. It seems that we are not moving. Our bodies, our senses, our bellies and tongues begin to scream at us "You hunger! You thirst! Eat!" We begin to question our motives, our movement ... the Hill.

As we turn and look back toward the Tree in the Garden, we no longer see PALE GAS, but fruit – ripe and inviting.

There is a lovely creature upon the Tree in the Garden beckoning us to "Come, eat." We glance toward the Hill — a dying man upon a Tree covered in darkness. Our body begins to come alive, our soul withers. We turn back, back toward the Tree in the Garden.

+ + +

Again in the Garden ...

Sick. Having eaten so much of the Fruit of the Tree in the Garden — Pride, Anger, Lust, Envy, Gluttony, Avarice, and Sloth — we are sick. The Garden no longer seems so filled with light. We have once again discovered that the fruit which says "Come" speaks a lie.

If this is so, what of the Tree on the Hill?

It seems to be dark, Hell. What of it? Must we go and see?

The man hangs there. Is he dead? Why does he look upon us so?

There is pity and love in his stare. Before we have strength or ability to suppress it, our soul says "Yes!" We hear — and suddenly, we are there, on the Hill, beneath the Tree.

Our eyes of Faith are opened and our spirit soars — for here on this Tree is the Fruit of Redemption, the First Fruit of God. God Incarnate.

The refreshment of our soul overshadows our bodily lusts and passions. We are at peace.

+ + +

Again in the Wilderness ...

We were too smart for the Hill. The dream must have worn off. Now, in the Wilderness, we are tired and hungry. O soul, where art thou?

Depression sinks in. It is lonely and arid in the Wilderness. We know that in the Garden there is an abundance of fulfilling things. In the Garden are fame, fortune, and power. In the Garden are sensual pleasures, passionate pastures, and delights for the eyes.

O, to be in the Garden.

As we enter the Garden, we again see the beautiful and inviting creature on the Tree. He assures us that we will not become sick. "Come, eat!" In an instant our soul cries out, "No!" Our bodies deny the hearing. Our bodies **know** better.

Better me, O Garden Tree. Better me, I beg of thee ...

+ + +

In the Wilderness ...

The Wilderness is not where we want to be. Yet every day finds us there with decisions to make.
We are in the Wilderness today with bruises. We were kicked out of the Garden. Did we kick ourselves out?

Anyway, we didn't want to leave. But our friends betrayed us.

There we were with all the powers one could ask for – and **Wham!** Betrayal. We lost all, in the Garden.

He's on the Tree. The Hill that looks like Hell. Bruised and empty, we've had it with the Garden. Our soul sighs, "Lord, forgive."

We are there, beneath the Fruit of the Tree on the Hill. Feeling betrayed from the bountiful, beautiful fruit of the Garden, we decided to partake of this food. It looks bitter, dying ... dead? Yet, behold, there is redemption thereon, for the fruits of this Tree are Humility, Patience, Chastity, Contentedness, Temperance, Liberality, and Diligence.

We look upon the Fruit, the man on the Tree. "May we stay here always, Lord?" With eyes of love he looks upon us and says, "I love you" ... and dies.

"No!" we cry.

Immediately we are transported to the Garden.

+ + +

In the Garden ...

In the Garden there is only life. The hill of death and doom seems to us now like a bad dream. We are thankful to be in the Garden. The beautiful and inviting creature tells us that the Tree in the Garden is known as the Tree of Life. After what we saw on the Hill, we believe him.

We then sink our teeth into a good-sized bit of sloth and decide to give the Hill no more thought. We lust for more, proud of our new-found life. We eat, and eat, and eat. A glutton never had it so good. It is easy, nay necessary, to be greedy in the Garden. Our avarice knows no bounds – we envy all. "I want it all!" we shout in anger.

We are clothed as royalty.

The beautiful creature in nowhere to be found. Does this mean? Of course.

We are in charge!

+ + +

Again in the Garden ...

Our soul alone in silence waits.

Something is not right. In the Garden, we think we have found Paradise. Yet why is our soul so unhappy? Can it not taste the fruit? Does it not feel the power? Is it not shining with the light of the Garden?

"No," says the soul. For a moment, our brain – even our body – agrees. But we **know** better.

"You have eaten of the Tree of the Knowledge of Good and Evil," says the soul. "This, says God, is forbidden."

Yet, we are in the Garden. "In the Garden, nothing is forbidden." The beautiful creature said so. And, besides, we **know** that the Tree in the Garden is the Tree of Life. It must be. For the man on the Tree on the Hill has died. A tree that ushers in death cannot bring life. This much we know. Therefore, this Tree, in the Garden must be ...

+ + +

In the Wilderness ...

It seems that every day we awake in the Wilderness. Then we must choose to either spend our time in the Garden or on the Hill.

Decisions, decisions, decisions ...

"I cannot do it alone." It was just a thought. Or did it come from deeper within? Whatever it was, it landed us on the Hill. But, immediately upon our arrival, we found that we were surrounded by blood. Just before we cried "No!" ... our souls fed on "faith, hope, love."

At rest in the Garden, we put such things out of our minds as we bask beneath the Tree.

+ + +

In the Garden ...

Knowledge.

Eating of the fruits of the Tree in the Garden, we find that we can't get our fill. "More, more, more!" we passionately cry. Though we tire of anger, it seems to be a constant, consistent emotion in our domain.

Lust, we find, leads to action. The deed being done, we lie alone wasted with grief and remorse; the cure for which we also seek upon the Tree in the Garden. The beautiful creature claims to have a remedy for all our ills.

This day, as we shrink from the fruit of lust, we are offered an orb of pride. The beautiful creature tells us that this fruit is the chief remedy of all ailments. "Taste and see," says he.

+ + +

On the Hill we sit ...

How we got here, we're not quite sure. Yet, we're thankful. For some odd reason, it seems that we've been sitting here beneath the Tree on the Hill ... staring off into space. And, oddly enough, this seems all right.

We remember that in the Garden we were clothed as royalty. Here, we sit in the shade of redemption – naked – with a cross. The man who led us here told us that we had to bear it if we were to find rest in him and his kingdom.

Funny, it seems that he met us in the Wilderness. We didn't have to make the decision to either go into the Garden or to climb the Hill. Instead, we were met by a man who seemed to know us – and, we him. He lovingly said, "Come, follow me." And now, here we are.

Where did he go?

Where is his kingdom?

Why did he call us?

+ + +

Again on the Hill ...

"Fear God and all will be well." There it is again —

"Fear God and all will be well" – that thought.

What does it mean to fear God? Why, how, is it that "all will be well?"

The man who brought us to the Hill has been gone for a long time. Perhaps it was all a dream, a hoax even? Maybe it would be better in the Garden. Had the man ever been to the Garden? Perhaps he led us the wrong way? Maybe he can be found in the Garden?

"No."

He clearly said that he was on his way to the kingdom. He bid us come, did he not? What was his name? "Fear God and all will be well. Fear God and all will be well. Fear God and all will be well ...."

"I fear that I am lost," we say. There, off in the distance, is the Garden. So inviting. So familiar. We've spent so much time there, in the Garden. It looks like home.

It is home. "Leave your cross and receive your crown, your reward," bids the creature.

So be it.

And it is so.

+ + +

In the Garden ...

It is easier in the Garden. The Hill involves sacrifice. For love requires that one give up self for other. Joy necessitates suffering. Peace implies war. Patience is ultra-sacrificial. And kindness quite often makes us nauseous!

Our taste buds dance as we bite again into the fruit of pride.

Yes, we eat it for a remedy. We were a little queasy last eve after a bout with envy and greed. It seems that we just can't get enough of the Garden. Now, here we sit partaking of the omnipotent medicine of pride.

From where we sit in the Garden we can see the weak and naked pilgrims ascend the Hill of Hell. Oh how our minds delight in hating them and their pitiful wasted lives. Wait till they get to the top and realize that death alone beckons and awaits them.

"He dies, you know!"

"He dies!"

Pride is abundant upon this Tree in the Garden.

+ + +

In the Wilderness ...

"Who am I?"

Tears. It's been long in coming – and still longer since last we cried. Once again we seemingly had it all in the Garden. Now all is lost. Again we were betrayed. It wasn't the fault of the creature, or the environment of plenty. It was the others who chose to inhabit the oasis of the Garden. Damn them!

Did they not know that "I am?"

"I'll show them!"

It was all to no avail – scheming and planning. They were too powerful. In fact, they've actually lived in the Garden a very long time. They **know** more. They've not only eaten fruit, they've stockpiled it in their paradisal warehouses. They were too powerful. We had to leave ... but, we shall return.

+ + +

Again in the Wilderness ...

"Don't want to go to the Hill. It involves commitment."

The Garden is much better. It requires nothing but our presence. The beautiful creature is a wonderful host. He is so smart, cunning, and encouraging. He makes us feel good, godlike.

We find the Hill generally depressing. "Except when there," whispers our soul – but, we know better. What good is a soul? Does it feed you? Thrill you? Does the soul ever dance, sing, or laugh?

Doubt.

Doubting in the Wilderness. We're tired. Our memory races toward the past: the man who claimed to be king, the sinful pleasures of the Garden. The bitter deeds brought on by the beautiful fruit. The dying man, the blood, the Tree. Which tree?

+ + +

Again in the Wilderness ...

We are beginning to get accustomed to the Wilderness. It isn't life. It isn't death. It just is.

We can see the Garden; the fruits – Life?

We can see the Hill; the Tree, the man – Life?

The questions plague us ... (till death do us part).

No. It is better to just stay in the Wilderness. Here there is no salvation or damnation. No Satan, sin, and death. No faith, hope, and charity. No day. No night. We're neither naked nor royally clothed. We are alone and at peace. The beautiful creature has journeyed with us into the Wilderness. All is well.

+ + +

Again in the Wilderness ...

The beautiful creature is a wonderful guide, very intelligent. He has taught us that we can partake of heavenly fruit – even in the Wilderness. All we have to do is to think. "Bring the fruit to mind." In so doing, we conjure up fantasy – lustful fantasy. We can build palaces of gold and silver, filled with riches, in our minds.

"Must we go back to the Garden?" we ask.

"No my child, you can have it all in the Wilderness."

We're no longer alone in the Wilderness ... thanks to the beautiful creature and the calf of gold.

+ + +

In the Garden?

It is hard to make out all that has happened; too much partying. Life's a blur. All is a blur. Our minds are clouded. Where are we?

Ahead, we see a shape. "Who's there?"

No answer. Can't be the creature – for he has an answer for everything!

We slowly approach. If our eyes don't deceive us, it looks like a tree.

Is it a tree?

Yes.

Is this tree, we now see, in the Garden? Or, is this the one on the Hill?

The calf only stares; the creature has disappeared.

There is no blood. There is no fruit.

It's only a dead and barren – lifeless – tree in the Wilderness.

With great fear we look around us. We are truly alone. No fantasies, no gold, no friends, no hope.

It's just us ... and a mirror.

A mirror.

We, the tree.

+ + +

Again on the Hill ...

The longer we stay here, the less we ask. The longer we stay here, the less we ask. The longer we stay here, the less we ask.

The longer we stay here, the more we find ourselves looking into the eyes of our beloved, the man on the Tree. Our souls seem wedded to his – and our bodies begin to obey our souls, his.

The question is: How is it that one is filled by emptying? How is it that one is happy yet crying? How is it that one is life-giving while dying?

The longer we stay here ...

The doubts. "If you are the Son of God, come down from the Cross and save yourself," a voice cries.

Our eyes must ask the question ... for he again, with love, dies.

+ + +

Again on the Hill ...

It seems that there are less people on the Hill today; more in the Garden.

We've stopped looking at the Tree on the Hill.

Everyone is happy, laughing, dancing in the Garden. There ring shouts of joy! In the Garden, where all is knowledge, there are no questions. The Tree is not stained with blood. There is life in the Garden.

It is *familiar.*

We can never get used to this Hill. It is too hard a thing for us. We were created to be in the Garden.

What awaits us here? Were we created to die?

"No."

+ + +

In the Garden ...

Friends! Ah, glorious friends! How we've missed you! The betrayals are forgotten. Let us eat, drink, and be merry!

In the Garden are many whom we know. They have welcomed us back to paradise with open arms, a warm embrace, and sweet caresses.

Lust tastes good as we feast upon the Tree. You'd think gluttony was our end! Alas, all the fruit is good and plenteous. Thanks be to God!

("No.")

For a moment, we thought we heard ... what?

A still small voice?

Must be the wine.

The homecoming is so overpowering that tomorrow we're planning a diet of sloth.

+ + +

Again in the Garden ...

Anger. Sometimes (do our eyes deceive us?) we seem to partake of anger by mistake. It often looks just like pride.

Since pride, we're told, is the omnipotent remedy for all our ills – we naturally reach for it daily.

Yet anger is found within.

"It is not anger. You are a god. You are in control. The world can be yours. Taste and see!"

The creature; we no longer see him. He just seems to accompany our thoughts, doubts, and fears.

For this we are thankful. Because on the Hill there are no answers ... only questions.

Mystery. Frustrating.

[Chomp!]

Anger? Pride? We've eaten too much sloth to care.

+ + +

In the Wilderness ...

Doubts. Funny. On the Hill our doubts are brought on by questions. In the Garden, they are due to answers received.

Whom to trust?

The more friends we found in the Garden, the lonelier we became. They became, like the fruit, too familiar. No mystery.

For the moment, we are content in the Wilderness. Someone holds our hand. We dare not look. We're afraid.

"All will be well."

"Trust me."

We do not look. Mystery. For now, it is good.

"Yes."

Who spoke?

... we are on the Hill.

+ + +

Again in the Wilderness ...

Our time on the Hill was very brief. We did not want to be there. But, because we trusted the voice in the Wilderness, there we were. But we did not want to be there.

We'd rather be alone. No one drove us into the Wilderness. We were not tempted. We made the decision all on our own. We are not headed back to the Garden. We just want to be alone.

Someone holds our hand. It is familiar ... it is okay.

+ + +

In the Wilderness?

The Creature. What would we do? Where would we be…
without him? He is so full of encouragement and
knowledge.

We may be moving soon … to the Garden. The creature
tells us that the Wilderness is actually part of the Hill.

"Unless you want to die, like him, you must flee the
Wilderness. You belong in the Garden. You were created
for the Garden, and the Garden for you. Yours is not to
die, but to live! How can you live without the plenteous
fruit of the Garden?"

We want so badly to trust.

Doubt. Friends. Betrayal. Sin?

We remember the past. Remorse.

+ + +

On the Hill …

An answer: "The key is not in the forgetting but in the
forgiving."

"This is too hard a thing for me, Lord. In the Garden,
when I forget, I am able to live! Here, when I try to
forgive, it seems that a part of me dies!"

Yes.

Patience. Long-Suffering. Peace. These live.

It seems that, on the Hill, with death there is new life.

The more we give, the more we gain. Forgiving is for getting.

+ + +

Again on the Hill ...

"He did not die."

It was but a voice, a thought. One not invited, but present nonetheless.

Of course he died ... we've seen it. We continue to see it. It is somehow connected with love. Love for us.

"It is a lie. He did not die. It is a myth. In fact, he never even lived. It is wishful thinking; nothing more."

For days now, these thoughts – little demons, they are – have been on attack. At the same time, we've discovered that if we do not wish to stay, he does *not* die. Well, not exactly.

We've discovered that when we say, "Lord, I want to stay here always" – he says, "I love you," and dies.

However, if we simply gaze upon his loving death on the Tree, we are filled with awe and wonder. We are filled.

Then, if we say, "Lord, I want to follow," the scene is transfigured. The Tree is replaced by an Empty Cave.

It is then that the little demons attack, just as we prepare to take our first step forward toward the new image.

"He died. He never lived. He died. He never lived. He died ...."

+ + +

In the Wilderness ...

Once again, we're uncertain of our location. We were on the Hill, preparing to enter the Cave, when all of a sudden our surroundings became hazy – clouded judgment?

A voice behind us says, "Turn back! You are lost!"

Ahead we hear, "Come."

"He died. He never lived ...."

Once again we are plagued with the familiar thoughts, doubts. We see a man dressed in white. He is very beautiful. "Whom do you seek?" he asks.

"The man ... the man on the Tree ....."

(He died. He died. He died. He died. Dead.)

As if he, too, could hear our legion of doubts, he replies, "Why do you seek the dead among the living? He is not here. He lives."

No.

+ + +

In the Garden ...

We're here only for a brief stay – just till we can clear our head and move on.

In the Garden, things make sense. In the Garden, all is rational, relative. We know that the dead don't live. We are smarter than that. Sure, we seek the truth. But truth must make sense! Truth should not – does not – contradict knowledge. Truth is rational.

The fruit is particularly tasty today. The color is a deep dark red. In fact, the fruit of the Tree looks like blood.

For a moment, our minds reel back to the Hill. We see OUR fruit in the palm of HIS hands. Nails!

We see him. We are no longer in the Garden.

+ + +

On the Way ...

A new path. The Wilderness reversed? The Garden is now to our right, the Hill to our left. We have turned around. We are following.

He did live. He did die. He now lives. We follow him ... out of the Wilderness.

We can go back to the Garden anytime.

We might be found under the Tree on the Hill from time to time.

He has warned us that the Garden leads to death. The beautiful creature is Evil Incarnate and a liar.

The Hill, though resembling death, leads to Life.

As we follow him, we are not alone. Others have gone on before.

Something is holding our hand. Or ... are we holding it?

A cross; it is a cross. Although comforting, it is **never** familiar.

(The cross is never familiar.)

+ + +

On the Way ...

The blood doesn't stain us. In fact, it seems to wash us. The fruits from the Garden are washed away by the Fruit of the Hill. The tree that we bear is our defense against the enemy, the evil one. We used to think him beautiful.

We now *know* ... **better**.

Knowledge: it's not all it's cracked up to be. Much of the experience of the Garden is knowledge. Where did it get us? Deeper into the Wilderness, farther from the Light, in the opposite direction of the Hill.

"Satan," they call him. He is very beautiful. Very sincere. Very attractive.

Very disguised.

And the fruits? They've been there always ... in the Garden. The Tree, however, is not that of Life. For, the Life-giving Tree is on the Hill. The Tree in the Garden is the same one that tempted Adam and Eve. The same Tree tempts us all. For the Tempter can always be found thereon.

They are not actually "fruits" at all ... but, seeds.

Seeds of evil.

When planted within us, we bear fruit. We, too, are trees.

+ + +

On the Way ...

Yes, we are trees, bearing fruit. Like the Tree in the Garden, we can bear sinful fruit: Pride, Anger, Lust, Envy, Gluttony, Avarice, Sloth. "Pale Gas" we call it. Fitting.

Or, if the seeds planted within us are done so by the Sower on the Hill, we bear fruit of a different kind: Humility, Patience, Chastity, Contentedness, Temperance, Liberality, and Diligence.

The knowledge gained in the Garden is self-serving and, therefore, self-condemning.

Deadly.

In the Garden, we learn how to place ourselves above others by putting them down. We are raised up at the expense of our neighbor.

On the Hill, we learn humility. This knowledge is God-serving. Therefore, it is life-giving. God is Life, God is Love. We learn how to serve our neighbor. In so doing, God is glorified. By our cross-bearing humility, we shall be raised up with Him at the Last Day.

There are still questions.

One has been entertaining us all the day long.
Was the Tree made for man? Or was man made for the Tree?

APPENDICES

Fr Joseph David Huneycutt

APPENDIX I

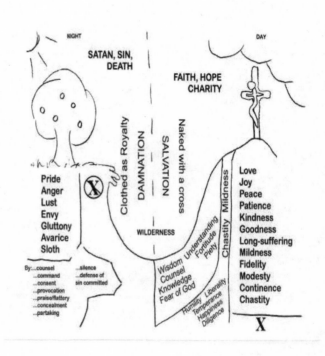

Fr Joseph David Huneycutt

APPENDIX II

Retreats & Workshops[185]

The background and resource material found in Part I coupled with the Meditations in Part II lend themselves well to a two-day Retreat. Here follows a journal entry concerning one such occasion, an example of what can be done within a group setting.

Friday

Following the gathering and worship, the retreatants met in the library of the monastery. Two easels with marker boards were set up to the right and left of the podium. These were used to draw the illustration of the Two Trees [Appendix I] and the various fruits mentioned in Chapter Two.

The first order of business for the Workshop was the obligatory personal introductions. This was followed by the reading of the story of the Fall as recorded in Genesis 3. What an effective discussion starter! We each shared our impressions and interpretations of the story of the Fall of Adam and Eve, going through the various "curses" which followed their transgression.

The participants then listed and defined, in their own words, the seven Passions and the corresponding Virtues. Since all of the participants were Christians accustomed to making regular Confession, many of the Passions were familiar to them. As is usually the case, it was much harder for the retreatants to list and define the Virtues; although the exercise was made easier by viewing

---

185 Please see Appendix III for a sample Retreat Schedule.

the Virtues as the opposite of the Passions. Lively discussion followed. These Passions (Pride, Anger, Lust, Envy, Gluttony, Avarice, and Sloth) were portrayed as fruit on the Tree of the Knowledge of Good and Evil. We then discovered their opposites, the Virtues.

The Virtues (Humility, Patience, Chastity, Contentedness, Temperance, Liberality, and Diligence) were listed on the board upon which was drawn an image of the Crucifixion. The most substantive portion of the workshop was the discussion of why it is that we seem more familiar with the Passions – the Tree of the Knowledge of Good and Evil – than with the Virtues and the Tree of Life. In other words, why do we spend so much time in the Garden of disobedience rather than on the Hill beneath the Cross of Christ? Of course, we spent more time talking about the Passions as the Retreat is designed to help one make a good Confession (wherein we confess our sins rather than our good works). The Virtues, on the other hand, should be our goal following the Confession of our sins. The Virtues are most likely that remedy which the Confessor exhorts the penitent toward.

This was a very sobering exercise which involved introspection and sharing of our personal lives. It led nicely to the conclusion of the Workshop, praying St Ephraim's Prayer together, and the service of Evening Prayer.

Saturday

On the morning of the second day, we gathered for Divine Liturgy. The participants were allowed to talk during the breakfast snack which followed. However, once we began the Meditations, silence was the rule of the day. (Many later commented on how difficult it was to keep silent.) Unlike the prior evening, we held the Meditations in the chapel. There was ample silence provided between each presentation which allowed for personal reflection and prayer. I had asked the participants to please refrain from excusing themselves from the assembly except during the brief pauses between talks. This helped to eliminate distractions and to keep everyone focused.

Following an hour-long (silent) break where participants were allowed freedom to read, pray, walk, etc., we gathered in the chapel for a sung service, the Akathist Hymn.[186] All were encouraged to participate in the service. This was a powerful experience, moving from silence to a service of sung worship.

During lunch, we ate in silence as someone read selections from *A Spiritual Psalter* by St Ephraim the Syrian. All of these activities were designed specifically to lead up to the final Meditation, "The Two Trees," which is the crown of the Retreat. Quiet time was provided after this to allow for Confessions. Following the Confessions, we gathered in the refectory (monastery dining hall) for concluding remarks, the dissemination of retreat evaluations, and prayers before dismissal.

---

186 An Akathist is a hymn of 24 stanzas honoring a Saint. We used the Akathist to Our Lady, the All-Holy Theotokos, "Quick to Hear."

Fr Joseph David Huneycutt

APPENDIX III

Retreat Schedule

Friday

4:00 pm – Gathering, Introductions, and Fellowship

5:00 pm – Prayer (Vespers, Vigil, etc.)

7:00 pm – Dinner

8:00 pm – "Two Trees" Workshop

10:00 pm – Prayers before bed (Evening Prayer, Compline, etc.)

Saturday

8:00 am – Prayer (Matins, Mass, Divine Liturgy, etc.)

9:30 am – Breakfast

10:00 am – Quiet Day Retreat begins / Meditations

11:30 am – Break

12:30 pm – Prayer (Akathist, Rosary, Hours, etc.)

1:30 pm – Lunch in silence (with readings)

2:00 pm – Final Meditation

4:00 pm – Confessions & Quiet Time

5:00 pm – Concluding remarks, end of Retreat

Though originally designed for Orthodox Christians, this Retreat is conducive to other liturgical groups, especially Roman Catholics, Anglicans, and Lutherans. Prayer services may vary; what is paramount is allowance of quiet time for reflection.

Readings during the Silent Lunch can be from *The Ladder of Divine Ascent*, *A Spiritual Psalter*, the Psalms, etc.[187]

For one-day Retreats, the Two Trees Workshop would be offered in the morning, followed by lunch and Meditations. Given the brevity of such a schedule, silence may not be desired or practical. Also, the "Two Trees" meditation may not be as effective within a short program.

---

[187] See Bibliography.

APPENDIX IV

What is Grace?

> *All of these items just mentioned are not fruits.*
> *They are beautiful green leaves that are needed*
> *only for the time being but that will one day*
> *wither and leave us naked in the fall of our life.*
> *Your soul, my dear one, is the branch, and the*
> *fruit that the vinedresser seeks is the amount of*
> *growth your soul has achieved in grace, as well as*
> *your promotion in the faculties of the spiritual*
> *life. Pay attention then and look for your fruits,*
> *lest the strength of the vine in you and the sap you*
> *have exhausted should be fruitless. Your end*
> *would then be to be cut off and used for fuel.* [188]

What, exactly, *is* "grace?" One popular and quick response refers to "saying Grace" before meals. Where does that come from? Most likely, the answer lies in the Latin – *gratias agere* – for "giving thanks" as in "Gratias Deo agamus" ("Let us give thanks to God"). Yet, thanking God and/or asking His blessing upon food at meal times does not answer the question. Other quick responses involve words such as *graceful* and *gracefully* – as in, she's a graceful dancer, or, he sure fell down gracefully. These words, which refer to beauty and form, still do not answer the question: What is grace?[189]

---

[188] Father Matta El-Meskeen (Matthew the Poor), *Orthodox Prayer Life – The Interior Way* (Crestwood, New York: St. Vladimir's Seminary Press, 2003), p. 198.

[189] For the purposes of this section, I have emphasized usages of **grace**.

Here's the definition from the Orthodox Study Bible:

GRACE: The gift of God's own presence and action in His creation. Through **grace**, God forgives sins and transforms the believer into His image and likeness. **Grace** is not merely unmerited favor – an attitude of God toward the believer. **<u>Grace is God's uncreated energy bestowed in the sacraments and is therefore truly experienced</u>**. A Christian is saved through **grace**, which is a gift of God and not a reward for good works. However, because **grace** changes a person, he or she will manifest the effects of **grace** through righteous living.[190]

It turns out that there are several meanings of the word **grace** in the Scriptures:

1) signifying the general mercy of God *(I Pet. 5:10)*
2) referring to the grace of Christ and the whole economy of salvation *(Eph. 2:8-9)*
3) referring to the gifts of the Holy Spirit which have been, and are being, sent down upon the Church for the sanctification of Her members

---

[190] See John 1:17; Rom 5:21; Eph 1:7; 2:8; 2 Thess 1:12; 1 Pet 5:5. *The Orthodox Study Bible* (Nashville: Thomas Nelson, 1993), pp. 799-800; emphasis mine.

It is this third understanding of **grace** (in Greek, *charis*) which the Apostles so often write about, and its use is identical with *dynamis* or **power**.[191]

St Symeon the New Theologian warns us that a Christian:

1) who does not bear in his heart the conviction that the **grace** of God, given for faith, is the mercy of God ...

2) if he does not labor with the aim of receiving the **grace** of God, first of all through Baptism, or ...

3) if he had it and it departed by reason of sin, to cause it to return again through repentance, confession, and a self-belittling life; and ...

4) if, in giving alms, fasting, performing vigils, prayers and the rest, he thinks that he is performing glorious virtues and good deeds valuable in themselves – then he labors and exhausts himself in vain.[192]

---

[191] See, for example: II Pet. 1:3, Rom. 5:2, Rom. 16:20, I Pet. 5:12, II Pet. 3:18, II Tim. 2:1, I Cor. 16:23, II Cor. 13:14, Gal. 6:18, Eph. 6:24, and other places.
- Michael Pomazansky, *Orthodox Dogmatic Theology*, trans. and ed. Seraphim Rose (Platina, California: St Herman of Alaska Brotherhood, 1997), p. 260.
[192] Pomazansky, pp. 260 - 261. **Note:** "**Providence** is what we call God's power in the world that supports the existence of the world, its life, including the existence and life of mankind and of each man; while **grace** is the power of the Holy Spirit that

Thus, **grace** is a strengthening – given by the Holy Spirit in His mercy and love to aid us in our struggle toward the Kingdom. We participate in **grace** by submitting our will to God's will, by trusting in Him. We commune with God through prayer and in the **grace-filled** sacraments of His Church. In essence, grace **is** the Holy Spirit.

> The advent and withdrawal of grace also has another saving characteristic. It comes for a while, cleanses man from a passion and goes. It comes again to cleanse him from another passion and so on, until man becomes able to purify the passive part of the soul, with the help of the divine and life-giving grace. After much struggle and many sacrifices, there comes a time when grace is stabilized, more or less, within the heart and then unbroken peace prevails! Constant calmness! Ever lasting sweetness! The soul becomes a Tabor! Heaven comes on earth! The Kingdom of God in the heart! The Holy Trinity within us! Man after the image and likeness of God![193]
>
> As you understand, my father, man is being continuously perfected and cleansed. The passive aspect of the soul is first cleansed and then the intelligent power of the soul. The faithful are initially

---

penetrates the inward being of man, leading to his spiritual perfection and salvation" (p. 261).

[193] NDHM, p. 108.

delivered from the passions of the flesh;
then – through harder prayer and more
intensive struggle, from the passions of
hatred, anger and rancour. When man
manages to be freed from anger and
rancour, it is obvious that the passive
aspect of his soul has almost been
purified. Then the entire warfare is carried
out in the intelligent aspect, and the
athlete wars against pride, vainglory and
against all vain thoughts. This warfare will
follow him to the end of his life. But all
this course of purification takes place with
the help and energy of grace so that the
faithful becomes a vessel receptive of rich
divine grace.[194]

We know from the teaching of our Holy
Fathers that virtues do not unite man
with God perfectly, but they create the
appropriate climate so that prayer comes
which unites man with God, the Holy
Trinity. Virtues are a prerequisite for the
granting of much grace, yet they also offer
grace.[195]

---

[194] NDHM, p. 113.
[195] NDHM, p. 53.

Fr Joseph David Huneycutt

APPENDIX V

Bless My Enemies, O Lord[196]

Bp. Nikolai Velimirovich

Bless my enemies, O Lord. Even I bless them and do not curse them.

Enemies have driven me into your embrace more than friends have. Friends have bound me to earth, enemies have loosed me from earth and have demolished all my aspirations in the world.

Enemies have made me a stranger in worldly realms and an extraneous inhabitant of the world. Just as a hunted animal finds safer shelter than an unhunted animal does, so have I, persecuted by enemies, found the safest sanctuary, having ensconced myself beneath your tabernacle, where neither friends nor enemies can slay my soul. Bless my enemies, O Lord. Even I bless them and do not curse them.

They, rather than I, have confessed my sins before the world.

They have punished me, whenever I have hesitated to punish myself.

---

[196] Reprinted from *Prayers by the Lake*, (pp.144-146) by Bishop Nikolai Velimirovich, by permission of the Serbian Orthodox Metropolitanate of New Gracanica, 1999, with blessing of His Grace, Bishop LONGIN.

They have tormented me, whenever I have tried to flee torments.

They have scolded me, whenever I have flattered myself.

They have spat upon me, whenever I have filled myself with arrogance.

Bless my enemies, O Lord, Even I bless them and do not curse them.

Whenever I have made myself wise, they have called me foolish.

Whenever I have made myself mighty, they have mocked me as though I were a dwarf.

Whenever I have wanted to lead people, they have shoved me into the background.

Whenever I have rushed to enrich myself, they have prevented me with an iron hand.

Whenever I thought that I would sleep peacefully, they have wakened me from sleep.

Whenever I have tried to build a home for a long and tranquil life, they have demolished it and driven me out.

Truly, enemies have cut me loose from the world and have stretched out my hands to the hem of your garment.

Bless my enemies, O Lord. Even I bless them and do not curse them.

Bless them and multiply them; multiply them and make them even more bitterly against me:

so that my fleeing to You may have no return;

so that all hope in men may be scattered like cobwebs;

so that absolute serenity may begin to reign in my soul;

so that my heart may become the grave of my two evil twins, arrogance and anger;

so that I might amass all my treasure in heaven;

ah, so that I may for once be freed from self-deception, which has entangled me in the dreadful web of illusory life.

Enemies have taught me to know what hardly anyone knows, that a person has no enemies in the world except himself.

One hates his enemies only when he fails to realize that they are not enemies, but cruel friends.

It is truly difficult for me to say who has done me more good and who has done me more evil in the world: friends or enemies.

Therefore bless, O Lord, both my friends and enemies.

A slave curses enemies, for he does not understand. But a son blesses them, for he understands.

For a son knows that his enemies cannot touch his life. Therefore he freely steps among them and prays to God for them.

Bless my enemies, O Lord. Even I bless them and do not curse them.

APPENDIX VI

Spiritual Helps and Christian Duties[197]

The Three Theological Virtues
Faith
Hope
Charity

The Four Cardinal Virtues
Prudence
Justice
Temperance
Fortitude

The Christian Duties
Prayer
Fasting
Almsgiving

The Seven Gifts of the Holy Spirit
Wisdom
Understanding
Counsel
Fortitude
Knowledge
Piety
Fear of God

---

[197] Taken from *The Practice of Religion* (New York: Morehouse-Gorham, 1944), pp. 80-83; and *A Pocket Prayer Book for Orthodox Christians* (Englewood, New Jersey: Antiochian Orthodox Christian Archdiocese, 1956), pp. 28-32.

The Fruits of the Holy Spirit
Love
Joy
Peace
Patience
Kindness
Goodness
Longsuffering
Mildness
Fidelity
Modesty
Continence
Chastity

The Seven Spiritual Works of Mercy
To instruct the ignorant.
To counsel the doubtful.
To correct offenders.
To endure injury.
To forgive wrong.
To pray for others.
To comfort the afflicted.

The Seven Corporal Works of Mercy
To feed the hungry.
To visit the sick.
To clothe the naked.
To help prisoners.
To shelter the stranger.
To bury the dead.
To visit the widows and the fatherless.

Nine Ways of Participating in the Sins of Others

By counsel.
By command.
By consent.
By provocation.
By praise or flattery.
By concealment.
By partaking.
By silence.
By defense of the sin committed.

Seven Stages of Sin

Suggestion
Pleasure
Consent
Act
Habit
Slavery
Spiritual blindness

The Marks of Real Repentance

In the Heart: Contrition.
In the Mouth: Confession.
In the Life: Amendment.

Fr Joseph David Huneycutt

BIBLIOGRAPHY

Andrew of Crete, St. *The Great Canon - The Work of Saint Andrew of Crete*. Jordanville, New York: Holy Trinity Monastery, 1992.

Basil the Great, St. *On the Holy Spirit*. Crestwood, New York: St. Vladimir's Seminary Press, 1980.

Brown, Raymond E., et al. (eds.). *The New Jerome Bible Commentary*. Englewood Cliffs, New Jersey: Prentice Hall, 1990.

Catholic University of America. *New Catholic Encyclopedia*. New York: McGraw-Hill, 1967.

Cleopa of Romania, Elder. *The Truth of Our Faith - Discourses from Holy Scripture on the Tenets of Christian Orthodoxy*, ed. Peter Alban Heers. Thessalonica, Greece: Uncut Mountain Press, 2000.

El-Meskeen, Father Matta (Matthew the Poor). *Orthodox Prayer Life – The Interior Way*. Crestwood, New York: St. Vladimir's Seminary Press, 2003.

Ephraim the Syrian, St. *A Spiritual Psalter or Reflections on God*, trans. Isaac Lambertson. Liberty, Tennessee: St John of Kronstadt Press, 1997.

Ephrem, Saint. *Hymns on Paradise*, trans. Sebastian Brock. New York: St Vladimir's Seminary Press, 1990.

Essey, Bishop Basil, comp. *The Liturgikon - The Book of Divine Services for the Priest and Deacon*, 2nd ed. Englewood, New Jersey: Antakya Press, 1994.

Freedman, David Noel, ed. *Anchor Bible Dictionary*. New York: Doubleday, 1992.

Gregory of Nyssa, St. *The Life of Moses*, trans. Abraham J. Malherbe and Everett Ferguson. New York: Paulist Press, 1978.

Hausherr, Irénée. *Spiritual Direction in the Early Christian East*, trans. Anthony P. Gythiel. Kalamazoo, Michigan: Cistercian Publications, 1990; original French edition, 1955.

Jeffrey, David Lyle. *A Dictionary of Biblical Tradition in English Literature*. Grand Rapids: Eerdmans, 1992.

Harakas, Stanley Samual. *Living the Faith: the Praxis of Eastern Orthodox Ethics*. Minneapolis: Light and Life Publishing Company, 1992.

Hopko, Thomas. *An Elementary Handbook on the Orthodox Faith*, Volume 4: *Spirituality*. New York: The Department of Religious Education, The Orthodox Church in America, 1976.

John Chrysostom, St. *On Marriage and Family Life* , trans. Catherine Roth and David Anderson. Crestwood, New York: St. Vladimir's Seminary Press, 1997.

John Climacus, St. *The Ladder of Divine Ascent*, trans. Lazarus Moore. Boston: Holy Transfiguration Monastery, 1979, revised.

John of Kronstadt, St. *MY LIFE in CHRIST or Moments of Spiritual Serenity and Contemplation, of Reverent Feeling, of Earnest Self-Amendment, and of Peace in God: Extracts from the Diary of St. John of Kronstadt*, trans. E. E. Goulaeff. Jordanville, New York: Holy Trinity Monastery, 1994.

Joseph the Hesychast, Elder. *Monastic Wisdom*. Florence, Arizona: St Anthony's Greek Orthodox Monastery, 1998.

Knowles, Archibald Campbell. *The Practice of Religion - A Short Manual of Instructions and Devotions*. New York: Morehouse-Gorham, 1950.

Leon-Dufour, Xavier. *Dictionary of Biblical Theology*. New York: Seabury, 1973.

Leon-Dufour, Xavier. *Dictionary of the New Testament*. San Francisco: Harper, 1983.

Lossky, Vladimir. *The Mystical Theology of the Eastern Church*. Crestwood, New York: St Vladimir's Seminary Press, 1976.

Manley, Joanna, ed. *Grace for Grace, The Psalter and the Holy Fathers*. Menlo Park, California: Monastery Books, 1992.

Manley, Joanna. *The Lament of Eve*. Menlo Park, California: Monastery Books, 1993.

Mantzarides, Georgios I. *The Deification of Man: St Gregory Palamas and the Orthodox Tradition*, trans. Liadain Sherrard. Crestwood, NY: St. Vladimir's Seminary Press, 1997.

Merriam-Webster's Collegiate Dictionary, 10th Edition. Springfield: Merriam-Webster, Inc., 1994.

Moulton, Harold K., ed. *The Analytical Greek Lexicon Revised.* Grand Rapids: Zondervan, 1978.

New Oxford Annotated Bible, Revised Standard Version. New York: Oxford University Press, 1977.

Nicene and Post-Nicene Fathers of the Christian Church, First Series. Grand Rapids: Eerdmans, 1988.

Nikodemos the Hagiorite, St. *Exomolegetarion - A Manual of Confession*, trans. Fr George Dokos. Thessalonica, Greece: Uncut Mountain Press, 2006.

Nikodimos and Makarios, Sts. *The Philokalia*, trans. and ed. G.E.H. Palmer, Phillip Sherrard, Kallistos Ware. London: Faber & Faber, 1984.

O'Connor, Flannery. *The Complete Stories.* New York: The Noonday Press, 1998.

Orthodox Study Bible. Nashville: Thomas Nelson, 1993.

Paisios of Mount Athos, Elder. *Epistles.* Thessaloniki, Greece: Holy Monastery of Evangelist John the Theologian, 2002.

Papadeas, George L., comp. *Greek Orthodox Holy Week and Easter Services*. Daytona Beach, Florida: Patmos Press, 1994.

Pocket Prayer Book for Orthodox Christians. Englewood, New Jersey: The Antiochian Orthodox Christian Archdiocese, 1956.

Pomazansky, Michael. *Orthodox Dogmatic Theology*, trans. and ed. Hieromonk Seraphim Rose. Platina, California: St Herman of Alaska Brotherhood, 1997.

Psalter According to the Seventy, trans. Holy Transfiguration Monastery. Boston: Holy Transfiguration Monastery, 1987.

Roberts, Alexander and James Donaldson, eds. *The Ante-Nicene Fathers*. Grand Rapids: Eerdmans, 1989.

Saint Augustine's Prayer Book (West Park, New York: Holy Cross Publications, 1967, revised).

Scupoli, Lorenzo. *Unseen Warfare: The Spiritual Combat and Path to Paradise*, ed. Nicodemus of the Holy Mountain, rev. Theophan the Recluse. Crestwood, New York: St. Vladimir's Seminary Press, 1997.

Sophrony (Sakharov), Archimandrite, *Words of Life*, trans. Sister Magdalen. Essex: Stavropegic Monastery of St. John the Baptist, 1996.

Symeon the New Theologian, St. *The First-Created Man: Seven Homilies by St. Symeon the New Theologian*, trans. Seraphim Rose. Platina, California: Saint Herman Press, 1994.

Tarazi, Paul and Paul Nadim. *Galatians, A Commentary.* Crestwood, New York: St. Vladimir's Seminary Press, 1994.

Thompson, Francis (1859-1907), "The Hound of Heaven" http://www.houndsofheaven.com/thepoem.htm (viewed 6/21/07).

Velimirovich, Bishop Nikolai. *Prayers by the Lake,* trans. and eds. Rt. Rev. Archimandrite Todor Mika, Very Rev. Dr. Stevan Scott. Grayslake, Illinois: Free Serbian Orthodox Diocese of the United States of America and Canada, 1989.

Vlachos, Hierotheos. *A Night in the Desert of the Holy Mountain,* trans. Effie Mavromichali. Greece: Birth of the Theotokos Monastery, 1991.

Vlachos, Hierotheos. *Orthodox Psychotherapy - The Science of the Fathers,* trans. Esther Williams. Greece: Birth of the Theotokos Monastery, 1994.

Vlachos, Hierotheos. *The Illness and Cure of the Soul in the Orthodox Tradition,* trans. Effie Mavromichali. Greece: Birth of the Theotokos Monastery, 1993.

von Balthasar, Hans Urs. *Presence and Thought - An Essay on the Religious Philosophy of Gregory of Nyssa.* San Francisco: Ignatius Press, 1995.

Webster's New Universal Unabridged Dictionary. London: Dorset & Baber, 1979.

Abbreviations

ANF - Roberts, Alexander & James Donaldson, eds., *The Ante-Nicene Fathers*, Volume 7. Grand Rapids: Eerdmans, 1989.

HOP - Ephrem, Saint. *Hymns on Paradise*, trans. Sebastian Brock. New York: St Vladimir's Seminary Press, 1990.

LDA - John Climacus, Saint. *Ladder of Divine Ascent*, trans. Lazarus Moore. Boston: Holy Transfiguration Monastery, 1970.

LOE – Manley, Joanna. *The Lament of Eve*. Menlo Park, California: Monastery Books, 1993.

MT - Lossky, Vladimir. *The Mystical Theology of the Eastern Church*. Crestwood, New York: St Vladimir's Seminary Press, 1976.

NDHM - Vlachos, Hierotheos. *A Night in the Desert of the Holy Mountain*, trans. Effie Mavromichali. Greece: Birth of the Theotokos Monastery, 1991.

OP - Vlachos, Hierotheos. *Orthodox Psychotherapy - The Science of the Fathers*, trans. Esther Williams. Greece: Birth of the Theotokos Monastery, 1994.

P&T - Balthasar, Hans Urs von. *Presence and Thought - An Essay on the Religious Philosophy of Gregory of Nyssa*. San Francisco: Ignatius Press, 1995.

PV3 - Nikodimos and Makarios, Sts. *The Philokalia*, volume 3, trans. and ed. G.E.H. Palmer, Phillip Sherrard, Kallistos Ware. London: Faber & Faber, 1984.

SAPB - *Saint Augustine's Prayer Book*. West Park, New York: Holy Cross Publications, 1967, revised.

SDECE – Hausherr, Irénée. *Spiritual Direction in the Early Christian East*, trans. Anthony P. Gythiel. Kalamazoo, Michigan: Cistercian Publications, 1990; original French edition, 1955.

TDOM - Mantzarides, Georgios I. *The Deification of Man: St Gregory Palamas and the Orthodox Tradition*, trans. Liadain Sherrard. Crestwood, New York: St. Vladimir's Seminary Press, 1997.

TFCM - Symeon the New Theologian, St. *The First-Created Man: Seven Homilies by St. Symeon the New Theologian*, trans. Seraphim Rose. Platina, California: Saint Herman Press, 1994.

UW - Scupoli, Lorenzo. *Unseen Warfare: The Spiritual Combat and Path to Paradise*, ed. Nicodemus of the Holy Mountain, rev. Theophan the Recluse. Crestwood, New York: St. Vladimir's Seminary Press, 1997.